THE LOVE SHACK

Books by Don Nori Sr.

Breaking Generational Curses

His Manifest Presence

How to Find God's Love

The Hope of the Nation That Prays

Romancing the Divine

Secrets of the Most Holy Place

Secrets of the Most Holy Place, Volume Two

Tales of Brokenness

The Angel and the Judgment

The Love Shack

The Prayer God Loves to Answer

AVAILABLE FROM DESTINY IMAGE PUBLISHERS

THE PLACE PEOPLE SEARCH FOR THAT
DRAWS THEM TO BEST-SELLING BOOKS LIKE
The Shack, The Love Dare, Woman, Thou Art Loosed!,
The God Chasers, Your Best Life Now, and others.

THE LOVE SHACK

DON NORI SR.

DESTINY IMAGE® PUBLISHERS, INC.

P.O. Box 310, Shippensburg, PA 17257-0310

"Speaking to the Purposes of God for This Generation and for the Generations to Come."

This book and all other Destiny Image, Revival Press, MercyPlace, Fresh Bread, Destiny Image Fiction, and Treasure House books are available at Christian bookstores and distributors worldwide.

For a U.S. bookstore nearest you, call 1-800-722-6774.
For more information on foreign distributors, call 717-532-3040.
Or reach us on the Internet: www.destinyimage.com.

ISBN 10: 0-7684-3055-0
ISBN 13: 978-0-7684-3055-4

For Worldwide Distribution, Printed in the U.S.A.

1 2 3 4 5 6 7 8 9 10 11 / 13 12 11 10 09

Contents

Which road leads to the Love Shack?
What will get you to where you want to go?
The best answer is based on the question:
Where do you want to go?

Chapter 1

WHAT MAKES A BEST-SELLING BOOK?

What are we *really* looking for in a best-seller? I think we're looking for answers to questions that many of us—millions of us—have about life now, and life after.

> I need wonder to explain what is going to happen to me, what is going to happen to us when this thing is done, when our shift is over and our kids' kids are still on the earth listening to their crazy rap music. I need something mysterious to happen after I die. I need to be somewhere else after I die, somewhere with God, somewhere that wouldn't make any sense if it were explained to me right now.
> —Donald Miller, *Blue Like Jazz*[1]

Current best-seller *Blue Like Jazz* addresses the gray area of Christian matter. Appealing to every person's deepest thoughts, desires, and hopes, this book raises spirit-probing questions that many don't dare ask—yet long to know the answers. Intellectual assent will no longer suffice. Reason does not provide rest for the soul. We long for more. We long for reality. We know deep down inside our hearts that we can touch eternity in this life. No amount of doctrinal drivel will change the reality of truth and passion. We want to touch God. Here. Now.

I don't just want to know what there is in the afterlife—that stuff is easy to believe since I will experience it after this life is over—but I find myself asking, "Is this all there is to Christianity? Do we give our hearts to the Lord for only the life to come? Are we really doomed to struggle with the fears of divine rejection, hopelessness, and near-eternal fatal sins our whole lives? I am here now to simply hang on until I die?" For me, it is hard to imagine that Jesus did all that He did just to populate Heaven. Surely there must be destiny, fulfillment, and happiness here in this life. Dare I hope for more?

The old traditional religious beliefs don't work for me anymore. I am certain you have heard some of them: Christians are not promised happiness, only joy. (Huh?) If you are even moderately wealthy, you cannot enter the Kingdom of God. Christians are doomed to suffer; it is our lot in life. (Hmmm. Can't wait!) God doesn't personally speak to believers anymore. (Great foundation for a relationship!) I am sure you can add to this dismal list of religious excuses for not experiencing the fullness of our salvation in this life as well as the next.

In William Young's popular novel *The Shack*, the author pulls our faith out of our brains and back into our hearts, the only place it can grow and prosper.

God's voice had been reduced to paper, and even that paper had to be moderated and deciphered by the proper authorities and intellects. It seemed that direct communication with God was something exclusively for the ancients and uncivilized, while educated Westerners' access to God was mediated and controlled by the intelligentsia. Nobody wanted God in a box, just in a book. Especially an expensive one bound in leather with gilt edges, or was that guilt edges? Freedom is an incremental process.[2]

Both of these books are written by men who challenge today's religious status quo, bringing readers to the edge of their "assigned" pews and leaving them wondering: *Is there something more? Is a deeper spiritual relationship possible? Is there a meaning and purpose to my life beyond working, eating, sleeping, dying? Am I really just a pawn, as the old clichés proclaim? Does anybody love me? Am I really alone? Can the divine affect my life here and now?*

I don't want to be a pawn or a tool or a vessel or a worker bee. I want to know that I am loved in this dimension and in every dimension through which I pass. I want to know that divine love can be felt, yes, felt from God directly to the depth of my soul in a tangible, recognizable way. I want to know that this divine love is not fickle and moody and subject to my failures and my mistakes. I don't need a god who is just like me, or any other human being for that matter, who is inherently off balance and skewed. I need the anchor for my soul to be just that, the anchor. I need God—who offers a steady, reassuring sense of love and commitment to me, even when I am not doing so well. This is the God whom I dare to love!

GOD'S UNCONDITIONAL LOVE

After 36 years of marriage to my extremely divine wife, Cathy, I can tell you that I have truly come to understand and experience God's love for me in a very real way through her. It is as though I stumbled into a relationship that was and still is much bigger and much more profound that I can ever comprehend—true love.

> Unconditional love is eagerly promised at weddings, but rarely practiced in real life. As a result, romantic hopes are often replaced with disappointment in the home. But it doesn't have to stay that way. —*The Love Dare*[3]

Love. What hasn't been written about love since the first writing utensil hit the first flat surface? Yet people still search for the answer to true love. *The Love Dare* was published in 2008 and has sold more than 300,000 copies; and at this writing, it is still going strong! Considering that most books sell an average of 9,000 copies, *The Love Dare* has been extremely successful. It was released in conjunction with the film *Fireproof*, about a marriage headed for divorce because of pornography, pride, and assorted sins that daily tempt many.

> The Love Dare starts with a secret. ... The secret is this: you cannot manufacture unconditional love (or *agape* love) out of your own heart. It's impossible. It's

beyond your capabilities. It's beyond *all* our capabilities. ... It's something only God can do.[4]

The thought of a happy home life has made this best-seller one that strikes a chord with old and young couples alike. Who doesn't want a relationship, a marriage, where love and contentment reign?

Interconnected with loving and needing to be loved, people are driven by the yearning to be valued—to have a purpose in life. Before we can be faithful and loving mates, we need to discover our inner, God-given purpose—our reason for existing.

THE MISSING LINK?

The title of the runaway best-selling book *The Purpose Driven Life* lured millions who longed to experience a life different from their current humdrum one—a *purpose*-driven life.[5] The title alone captured the spirits and imaginations of more than 25 million people worldwide—all because they wanted to know that their lives count for something, to know that they have a reason for being in the "here" and the "now."

> ABC News [reported that] "*The Purpose Driven Life* is the epicenter of a spiritual shockwave taking root across America in unlikely places like offices and university campuses. It has become a movement."[6]

As well-known as this book and the author have become, there is a missing link. The concept is unforgettable, but the reality of a purposeful life remains a mystery—an enigma. This is unfortunate, as Scripture offers so much more for us. Our Lord is a relentless gatherer, "O Jerusalem, Jerusalem! You kill the prophets. God sent you His men, but you stoned them to death. I have often wanted to gather up your people, as a hen gathers up her baby chicks under her wings, but you refused" (Matt. 23:37). He is the One who sends, "I sent them into the world, just as You sent Me into the world" (John 17:18). He is the One who gives purpose and fulfillment, "...Lord, who else is there to go to? You have the words of eternal life!" (John 6:68). And we proclaim Him, admonishing every man and teaching every man with all wisdom, that we may present every man complete in Christ. (See Colossians 1:28.)

Fulfillment is experienced only when you are living out the purpose for which you were born.

The question of the moment, therefore, is most urgent. Is it fulfilling enough to know there is purpose, or does fulfillment actually require experiencing our God-given purpose in our lives? I am often called a mystic, but here I am truly a pragmatist: fulfillment is experienced only when you are living out the purpose for which you were born. In most instances, there are several purposes to be fulfilled in one's lifetime. Just knowing this is true, however, without stepping into those purposes would seem to me to be most frustrating, indeed.

My little children, again I feel pain for you, such as a mother feels when she gives birth to her child. I will feel this, until Christ is fully formed in you (Galatians 4:19).

This is what I am working for. Using all the energy that He exercises so powerfully in me, I am struggling to do this (Colossians 1:29).

When the power of the Holy Spirit is moving within us, it is as though we are, as Paul describes it, "in labor." It is an overpowering, consuming, demanding force that requires our undivided attention toward action. This is something that mere intellectual understanding or doctrinal acceptance cannot fathom. The missing link is the Person of Jesus Himself, living, moving, and having His way accomplished in us. Not only does He love us, but He also has a real, definable purpose for our existence. His love draws us, His power prepares us, and His Holy Spirit leads us in wisdom, knowledge, and fulfillment.

But the actual mysteriousness of life is sometimes enough of a draw for readers. For instance, a few years before *The Purpose Driven Life* became "a movement," the best-selling *Left Behind* series sold more than 60 million copies worldwide. "Based on the prophecies in the Book of Revelation," these novels "chronicle the lives of those left behind after the sudden disappearance of millions of Christians." *Left Behind* generated reader mania for Christian fiction, "sparking nationwide interest in End-Times events, and generating intense media coverage."[7]

As with *The Purpose Driven Life*, many book clubs and discussion groups sprung up to consider the premise of the *Left Behind* series—pros and cons. But I believe the core of the books and the discussions (private and corporate) is the fact that people want to know if they will have a second chance after "the rapture"—will they really be condemned to hell if they miss the rapture boat?

If there is any doubt in a person's mind where they will end up after death, the *Left Behind* books give them hope that they could redeem themselves once and for all. For far too many, the total and complete redemption that Jesus provided on the Cross seems just too simple to accept. The ingrained work-hard-for-what-you-want ethic in most Americans actually hinders many from accepting God's free gift of salvation because they feel they must somehow work for it. As protagonists in the books work to spread the Gospel from underground and destroy the evil pervading the world, readers are drawn into their quest and identify with their struggle.

WHAT DO WE HAVE IN COMMON?

Tommy Tenney's *God Chasers* books are also read with great anticipation. He focuses on a particular insight:

> God chasers have a lot in common. Primarily, they are not interested in camping out on some dusty truth known to everyone. They are after the fresh presence of the Almighty. Sometimes their pursuit raises the eyebrows of the existing church, but usually they lead the church from a place of dryness back into the place of His presence. If you're a God chaser, you won't be happy to simply follow God's tracks. You will follow them until you apprehend His presence.[8]

Rebellion against the "same old" is a recurring theme in these best-selling books. People instinctively identify with rebels—people who go against the mainstream of things. Case in point, the wildly successful television show *The Sopranos.* The mystery surrounding wealthy crime families captures the imagination.

Likewise, appealing to the mysteries of Christianity intrigues and stirs the spirit. The inner longing of all people is met in Christ. No one is intrigued by the routine, the ordinary—that we take for granted. We search for more.

Knowing deep down that there is more is the focus of *Waking the Dead* by John Eldredge. His best-seller purports that "once the 'eyes of our hearts' are opened, we will embrace these eternal truths:

- Things are not what they seem.

- This is a world at war.

- Each of us has a crucial role to play.

- A battle is raging.

- And it is a battle for your heart."[9]

Again the mystery of God and His divine love for us is the hook that pulls people in. A spiritual battle for the heart with eyes to see, an unseen world at war, and our role in it. Where do we fit? How can we find our place in His plan?

This is certainly why C.S. Lewis' *Mere Christianity* has been read by millions over the past 50-some years.

If any topic could be relied upon to wreck a book about "mere" Christianity—if any topic makes utterly unprofitable reading for those who do not yet believe that the Virgin's son is God—surely this is it.[10]

LOOKING FOR OUR UNIQUENESS

Christian writers and publishers capture, harness, and redirect imaginations toward rebels *with* a cause like Martin Luther, Dietrich Bonhoeffer, or even Robin Hood, to move people toward God and His unique plan for them. Deep down, people like to think of themselves as individually special. We like to see ourselves as having unique thoughts and ideas—most of us actually do. Those who choose to act on them, write them, or put them into practice become much more fulfilled, and are a step closer to their destiny than those who dismiss their uniqueness or shelve their thoughts and ideas for later. Anyone can step away from the predictable, the common, or the mundane.

[Allow me to interrupt myself for a moment. Here we must see the difference between being fulfilled and just being content with holding radical beliefs, whether or not we actually act upon them. Fulfillment is not found only in intellectual assent of a belief; rather, it is *acting* upon that belief that turns a mere notion into a dynamic and often life-changing course of action. An old friend once told me that there is only one difference between a millionaire and one who struggles to pay his bills all his life. That difference is the willingness to act on an idea, a hunch, a belief. If you are willing to step out into the things of God that you know to be true, you will experience fulfillment.]

Anyone who has taken a sociology class knows that humans are creatures of habit and can be clumped together according to those habits. Accurate predictions can be made regarding actions and reactions when it comes to certain situations. For instance, American drivers, for the most part, drive on the right side of the road, obey traffic signals, and park between the white lines in the grocery store parking lot—these are good things. When we read about someone being maimed or shot as a result of "road rage," we are confounded. And who can forget hearing or reading about the "evil Santa" who killed eight on Christmas Eve in 2008? We often find ourselves wondering what happens to a person who becomes so out of control.

SOJOURN THROUGH LIFE

Everyone is on a journey. God designed each of us to walk through life with Him. Without Him, there is only chaos and disappointment. As we are one family, we have many of the same inherent traits, including:

- Wanting to be loved.

- Feeling broken and lost.

- Being restored and redeemed.

- Being called; having a unique mission and purpose.

- Feeling fulfilled.

- Being happy, content, satisfied.

Tying all these stepping stones together is the mortar of hope. Hope moves us into the future. Without hope, people—including Christians—become stagnant, purposeless.

HOPE IS TANGIBLE

Max Lucado, who has 40 million books in print, gives readers hope through providing modern-day biblical solutions to conquering demons such as debt, disaster, dialysis, divorce, deceit, disease, and depression. His practical principles reach into the "todays" of readers. Even his book titles ignite readers' expectations:

- *Facing Your Giants: A David and Goliath Story for Everyday People*

- *For These Tough Times: Reaching Toward Heaven for Hope and Healing*

- *3:16 The Numbers of Hope*

- *Cure for the Common Life: Living in Your Sweet Spot*

- *Traveling Light: Releasing the Burdens You Were Never Intended to Bear*

Weaving hope into our lives propels us forward on our journey. As authors find glimpses of truth along the way, they share their experiences; and when they resound in enough hearts and spirits, readers by the millions are enthralled.

Less-recent best-selling Christian authors include John Bunyan, Hannah Hurnard, C.S. Lewis, Oswald Chambers, Norman Vincent Peale, Billy Graham, Charles Spurgeon, Dietrich Bonhoeffer, and Augustine. Books by these writers are still read and often referred to today.

Weaving hope into our lives propels us forward on our journey.

The Pilgrim's Progress used to be required reading in some classrooms because of its rich descriptions and thoughtful dialogue. John Bunyan's classic was first published in 1678 and is still known worldwide as the most successful allegory ever written.[11] Not unlike the pilgrim's journey to the Celestial City, our journey too is pitted with characters who help and hinder. We can relate to Faithful, Vanity, Flatterer, and the Slough of Despair. Jim Pappas' adapted book takes Christiana, the pilgrim's wife, on a journey from the City of Destruction to the same City her husband sought.[12] All along the way, both Christian and Christiana are confronted with situations that cause the reader to identify, commiserate, and rejoice with the pilgrims.

Although written almost 60 years ago (as of this writing), two of C.S. Lewis' books in The Chronicles of Narnia series have recently been released as films by Disney: *The Lion, the Witch, and the Wardrobe* (which grossed $745 million in 2005) and *Prince Caspian*. As most of us can attest, the mystery behind the wardrobe doors creates intrigue that excites young and old. And what little guy doesn't want to be a prince? Even the word *prince* throws the mind into the realm of royalty where needs are immediately met, food is plentiful and delicious, and people live to serve you.

When reading a good book, gone are the dirty dishes, the honey-do list, the stale television shows, the too-tall grass. You are imagining another world—a world that you hope and pray ends happily.

Walt Disney's tales have been successful for generation after generation, and almost all of them end with "and they lived happily ever after." Curmudgeons have scoffed at this ending, but for Christians who know the ending is eternal life with God, this conclusion is not a fairy tale but a reality. Christians know that when we allow God to control the circumstances and trust His answer for the outcome, happy endings are inevitable.

Some books aim to relieve our insatiable curiosity about the afterlife or "other worldly" events; books that provide glimpses into the future are ever popular.

> An extraordinary true story of death, heaven, and a return to life on earth. Offers comfort and hope to those facing loss or uncertainty. —Don Piper, *90 Minutes in Heaven: A True Story of Death and Life*[13]

"To those facing loss or uncertainty." Those few simple words resonate in a person's soul—for we all face loss or uncertainty throughout our lives. Who doesn't want to be comforted and hopeful during those times, and all the time?

Marketers know this intrinsic spirit of ours and bank on it. Drug companies realize the potential of this vulnerability in our character and promise miracle cures for common aches and pains. Retailers count on it with every "You deserve it" sales pitch for things unnecessary. Weight loss pills and programs appeal to the need to look like the supermodel on television and in magazines. QVC spins once-in-a-lifetime offers to spark a sense of urgency.

When facing "loss or uncertainty," hope is the thread that holds us together.

John Eldredge's *Wild at Heart* has sold more than 2 million copies. The subtitle, *Discovering the Secret of a Man's Soul,* gives away the focus. He claims that "most Christian men are...bored" and "invites men to recover their masculine heart." He must have hit on a truth as 2 million people have bought the book to find out why and how. *Wild at Heart* is a best-seller providing hope.

With hope comes the audacity of wanting to be loved. Hope opens people to possibilities. Yes, I am loveable because God loves me—He sent His Son to be my Brother. A brother who loves me beyond death.

WANTING TO BE LOVED

> Love as distinct from "being in love" is not merely
> a feeling. It is a deep unity, maintained by the will
> and deliberately strengthened by habit; reinforced
> by the grace which both partners ask, and receive
> from God. They can have this love for each other

even at those moments when they do not like each other; as you love yourself even when you do not like yourself. —C.S. Lewis[14]

When you know that language, it's easy to believe that someone in the world awaits you, whether it's in the middle of the desert or in some great city...without such love, one's dreams would have no meaning. —Paulo Coelho, *The Alchemist: A Fable About Following Your Dream*[15]

Love works. It is life's most powerful motivator and has far greater depth and meaning than most people realize. It always does what is best for others and can empower us to face the greatest of problems. We are born with a lifelong thirst for love. Our hearts desperately need it like our lungs need oxygen. Love changes our motivation for living.[16]

I daresay all of the great writers of all time have written about love—a subject so deep and wide that it could be written about every day for eternity and still not have its breadth covered. Even apostle Paul devoted an entire chapter in First Corinthians to it and barely scratched the surface of its real power and eternal significance.

Is it so deep and formidable that we can't attain it? So precious that we are unable to possess it? So fragile that we can't maintain it? I think not. The consuming of Jesus Christ results in a love that is not only attainable, but a love that God fully expects us to embrace in ways we cannot begin to imagine.

During my journey to the Love Shack I've written several books that helped explain to others, as well as helped me determine, what was happening in my heart.

FEELING BROKEN AND LOST

In a world where religion seems to grow increasingly irrelevant *The Shack* wrestles with the timeless question, "Where is God in a world so filled with unspeakable pain?"[17]

> When the first couple chose to take action after being tempted, it caused all of us to be broken and lost. Sometimes those feelings are too hard for some to live with and the suicide talliers add another tick to the chart. More than 32,000 people ended their lives in the United States in 2004.[18]

Others, feeling broken and lost, instead turn to temporary relief—drugs (legal and illegal), alcohol, pornography, affairs, overeating, and the like. Some of the best-sellers tune in to these feelings and attempt to identify them, resonating in the readers' spirits.

> It was as if we were broken, I thought, as if we were never supposed to feel these sticky emotions. It was as if we were cracked, couldn't love right, couldn't feel good things for very long without screwing it all up. We were like gasoline engines running on diesel. I was just a kid so I couldn't put words to it, but every kid feels it. (I

am talking about the broken quality of life.) A kid will think there are monsters under his bed, or he will close himself in his room when his parents fight. From a very early age our souls are taught there is a comfort and a discomfort in the world, a good and bad if you will, a lovely and a frightening.[19]

The world's greatest lie: At a certain point in our lives we lose control of what's happening to us and our lives become controlled by fate.[20]

Some who are broken and lost turn to God, the church, the Bible, or to Christians for relief. Sometimes that works. Unfortunately, sometimes it doesn't.

Every blessing ignored becomes a curse. I don't want anything else in life. But you are forcing me to look at wealth and at horizons I have never known. Now that I have seen them, and now that I see how immense my possibilities are, I'm going to feel worse than I did before you arrived. Because I know the things I should be able to accomplish, and I don't want to do so.[21]

BEING RESTORED AND REDEEMED

If you're fortunate enough to live, mostly unscathed, through love betrayed and the misery of feeling broken and lost, your journey opens to a beautiful world of light and life. Your eyes open to sights never before imagined. Dreams are remembered; love is real; thoughts are clear; life is vivid and exciting; meaningful destiny is within reach!

> "You came so that you could learn about your dreams," said the old woman. "And dreams are the language of God. When he speaks in our language, I can interpret what he has said. But if he speaks in the language of the soul, it is only you who can understand."[22]

A life restored and redeemed is a life full of potential. Oh how we love to read about men and women who have made a difference by being good, decent people.

> Tony Dungy's words and example have intrigued millions of people, particularly following his victory in Super Bowl XLI, the first for an African American coach. How is it possible for a coach—especially a football coach—to win the respect of his players and lead them to the Super Bowl without the screaming histrionics, the profanities, and the demand that the sport come before anything else? How is it possible for anyone to be successful without compromising faith and family? In this inspiring and reflective memoir...Coach Dungy tells the story of a life lived for God and family—and challenges us all to redefine our ideas of what it means to succeed.[23]

CALLED — YOUR UNIQUE MISSION AND PURPOSE

It is always the simple things that change our lives. And these things never happen when you are looking for them to happen. Life will reveal answers at the pace life wishes to do so. You feel like running, but life is on a stroll.[24]

Knowing we are called for a greater purpose, for the greater good, for a greater God, gives us the strength and power we need to forge ahead in life. Forge ahead toward the Love Shack.

I knew God had called me to a powerful, worldwide ministry. I didn't brag about it and didn't feel that I was special. I knew I was just a woman from Fenton, Missouri, whom no one had ever heard of. Yet I believed I would have a national radio ministry. I believed God would use me to heal the sick and to change lives. —Joyce Meyer, *Battlefield of the Mind*[25]

Everyone dreams of being great, and there is nothing evil in that desire. We all want to be part of something significant. This is perfectly natural. Such a desire comes from God, because He created us for greatness.... First, you must find your gift; discover it. Second, you must define your gift; understand it. Third, you must refine your gift;

begin using it in small ways faithfully, and in larger ways as the Lord gives you opportunity. This means distributing your gift for free; giving it away. . . . the King will be watching and will reward you. —Myles Munroe, *God's Big Idea*[26]

On your journey to the Love Shack, you will find your gift, you will become part of something significant, and you will enjoy freely sharing your gift with all who are feeling broken and lost. In turn, your kindness and Christlike behavior will bring along more who are searching.

FEELING FULFILLED

God really does have unclaimed blessings waiting for you, my friend. I know it sounds impossible— even embarrassingly suspicious in our self-serving day. Yet that very exchange—your want for God's plenty—has been His loving will for your life from eternity past. And with a handful of core commitments on your part, you can proceed from this day forward with the confidence and expectation that your heavenly Father will bring it to pass for you. —Bruce Wilkinson, *The Prayer of Jabez: Breaking Through to the Blessed Life*[27]

Bruce Wilkinson's small—4½" x 6½"; 93 pages—book was a #1 *New York Times* best-seller and sold 9 million copies. Based on an Old Testament passage, First Chronicles 4:9-10, the wisdom in this book sheds light on God's desire to bless His people. "*. . . and*

God granted him what he requested." Could it be that easy? Millions bought the book to find out.

> This pile of bones had a potential that Ezekiel couldn't see, just as you have unseen potential. No matter what others say, God sees incredible potential in you. The Word of God says you're capable. Within you is an army. You merely need to dispel satan's fear and allow the wind to breathe upon that which God has formed in you. —T.D. Jakes, *Release Your Anointing*[28]

Bishop Jakes started a church in 1979 in West Virginia with ten members. He now pastors an interracial congregation of more than 30,000 in Texas. Humble beginnings move toward fulfillment of a God-given destiny.

God places a fulfilling destiny within each of His children. Total fulfillment is felt and lived only when we are walking and talking within His plan for our lives. But knowing this plan is not as initially important as believing that God has such a plan. Trusting Him for the destination brings confidence and peace. Like traveling with someone else leading the way, you will soon recognize where you are at and where you are going by the scenery, even if your destination was not known when the journey began.

Remember that we are always moving. Our lives are a journey with the map laid out by our Lord Himself. When we can rise each morning with confidence that He is the wagon master and He knows the way, we receive great peace. Stress is reduced the more we understand that He will carry us to the places of our adventures. The journey itself teaches us discernment, submission to His will, and humility, as well as all the lessons we need to accomplish the goals of our adventures. This, truly, is our peace.

BEING HAPPY, CONTENT, SATISFIED

If they obey (listen) and serve (worship) [Him], then they will be successful for the rest of their lives. And, the rest of their years [will be] happy (Job 36:11).

God convicted me of negative thinking. He taught me that if I would stop looking at the hardships and obey Him, He would make a way for me. [The Bible] tells us that God wants to bless us and prosper the work of our hands, but we must obey His commandments. ... He assures us that we can do it: "For this commandment which I command you this day is not too difficult for you nor is it far off."[29]

Those who revere the Always-Present One will live and be content, unbothered by trouble (Proverbs 19:23).

God is realistic. He knows that ecstasy is not an option; we are made for bliss, and we must have it, one way or another. He also knows that happiness is fragile and rests upon a foundation greater than happiness. All the Christian disciplines were formulated at one time or another in an attempt to heal desire's waywardness and so, by means of obedience, bring us home to bliss. . . . faith on its way to maturity moves from "duty to delight." If it is not moving, then it has become stagnant. If it has changed the goal from delight to duty, it has gone backward; it is regressing. This is the great lost truth of the Christian faith, that correction of Judaism made by Jesus and passed on to us: the goal of morality is not morality—it is ecstasy. You are intended for pleasure![30]

Always be happy in the Lord. Again I say, be happy! Show a gentle spirit to everyone. The Lord is near. Don't worry about anything. Instead, let God know what you are asking for in prayer. Tell Him all about what you want. And, be thankful (Philippians 4:4-6).

What does being happy, content, and satisfied mean to me? Realizing God loves me. I wrote the following a few years ago and it holds true today:

Thank God! He loves me, little ole me. He wants me. It does not matter what the religious right or the religious left may say. I am loved and there is nothing that can separate me from that love. Now that I have found Him whom my soul doth love, I will not run *to* Him; I will run *with* Him. I will not work *for* Him; I will work *with* Him. I will not worship to *get* His attention. I will worship because

I *have* His all. I won't worship to *gain* His favor but because I *have* His favor. I know I am in the palm of His hand. I know He has my life under His control. —Don Nori Sr., *Romancing the Divine*[31]

I feel sure of this one thing: The One who began a good work among you will continue it until it is finished, when Christ Jesus comes (Philippians 1:6).

Yes, the Always-Present One brought us out of there. He wanted to bring us [here] *to give us the land which He vowed to our ancestors* (Deuteronomy 6:23).

To me, that truth remains the foundation of happiness and joy eternal. It is absolutely critical that we understand this. All He has promised us, He intends to do for us. Right here on this earth. Right now in your life.

You will not allow Your Holy One to experience corruption. You will show me the pathway to life. Being with You will fill me with joy. At Your right hand I will find pleasure forever (Psalm 16:11).

My friends, welcome to the Love Shack!

Chapter 2

THE LOVE SHACK

The front door bangs open. "Hi Pap Pap! It's me!" The patter of little feet brings a smile to my face as Donnie the third runs into the den. He jumps on my lap, sending my book, notepad, pen, and television remote flying in all directions. "I miss you, Pap Pap," he says as he lays his head on my shoulder. He takes a deep breath and doesn't move.

"I know, Donnie. I miss you too."

Nearly every time before I go on a long trip, my grandchildren come to our home to say good-bye. It is not really necessary, but it is a good excuse to see them and let them climb all over me. They are truly medicine to my soul. Instead of aspirin when I have a cold, the doctor tells me to "take two grandchildren and call me in the morning." They are great.

Last November I was going to take a trip to Red Deer, Alberta, Canada. A few days before the trip when the grandchildren were visiting and playing around me, I told 4-year-old Alyssa that I would be very close to the North Pole. "If I see Santa, I'll tell him what good children you have been this year." She smiled weakly and walked away without response. I thought that a bit strange, but didn't give it another thought.

The time together was wonderful. Dinner, playing, laughing, plenty of toys—all the things that make Grandma's house a destination they love. But sadly the evening came to a close all too soon for me. Just before Alyssa walked out the door, she gave me a big hug and kiss. Then she stopped and looked at me very seriously, "Pap Pap, I think it would be better if you didn't mention me at all to Santa."

"What!?" I said to her, laughing.

"Pap Pap," she started reluctantly, "I wasn't very good this year. It's better if we don't remind him of it." Her beautiful, big brown eyes looked at me quite repentantly. I gathered her into my arms and hugged her with the reassurance that if Santa wouldn't bring her anything, Pap Pap would get her whatever she wanted.

This true incident reveals a lot about us as human beings. We know we are broken. We know we are needy. We know we fall short. And like my little granddaughter, there seems to be nothing we can do but accept our lot in life as not measuring up to the standards that we are expected to maintain. Thank God her parents are showing her the love of Jesus and the forgiveness He has for her. She will grow up understanding God's mercy and she will know the Lord as the loving heavenly Father that He is.

But for us, it takes more time to unlearn what we should never have been taught. As we grow older, though, we begin to understand that we can change. Most of us really want to change; we want to improve. We want to be fixed. We want to be effective and pleasing to the Lord Jesus. This is the main reason certain books sell so well. Something within us knows, hopes, or wants to hope that if we search for the clues to lasting change, we can actually experience it.

FINDING GOD'S RESTING PLACE

This is where the Love Shack comes into the picture. Let's admit it; we all want to have God's love in our lives. Most of us want to know that we are pleasing God daily. But it is also true that most of us do not think that we please Him or that there is anything we can do to be pleasing to Him every day.

We look to books for help. At the end of the day, the books that are usually the most popular are the ones that seem to be the most helpful to us. These books are all part of our journey to the Love Shack—the place of uncontested favor and acceptance. It is the place where mere mortals can rest in the peace and assurance that they are certainly accepted in the Lord and gathered into His family for blessing, care, favor, protection, and strength.

The Love Shack is the place where destiny is discovered and hope is revived.

The Love Shack is the place where destiny is discovered and hope is revived. Of all the places in time or out of time, in this dimension or any other, the Love Shack is the place where we can completely rest in His love. The Love Shack is where God rests too.

It is where He is always available and always ready for us to enjoy His Presence.

But there is more to the Love Shack than just acceptance, rest, and favor. It is also the place of healing—physical, mental, and spiritual. It is the place of sending, destiny, and purpose. It is where the Lord Jesus Himself pours His Holy Spirit over us, in us, and through us, bringing the wholeness we seek and the freedom from fear and torment that we so desperately need. Yes, the Love Shack is certainly the place of our hearts' desire and the place of His restorative Presence.

Our search begins right where we are in life and reaches its full impact in the Love Shack. Our journey continues there as we live with His Presence. There, our adventure with Him carries us through every broken, uncertain place in our hearts, healing, resolving conflicts, granting wisdom, and giving us a new beginning every morning. It refreshes, encourages, and blesses. This is the place Jesus called us to when He declared so long ago:

> *There are many rooms in My Father's house. I would have told you, if that were not true. I am taking a trip to prepare a place for you. Since I am leaving to prepare a place for you, you can be sure that I will come back and take you with Me, so that you will be where I am* (John 14:2-3).

The Love Shack is the holiest place in the entire universe. It is a special place for only you and your Lord. Angels literally stand guard and prevent anything from entering that is contrary to God's purposes for you. This is the place where all that is evil, destructive, and hateful is excluded. The Love Shack is where our uninterrupted fellowship with God is as common and anticipated as the rising sun. Common, yes, but not so common as to be taken advantage of. Common in that it is normal, expected, and celebrated as a daily, moment-by-moment reality in our lives.

NONCONDITIONAL UNCONDITIONAL LOVE

I have discovered unconditional love in the Love Shack. This is my personal place of refuge, hope, and confidence. For in the Love Shack, He comforts me and assures me that I can trust Him for His will. I don't confuse myself with religious terms such as "permissive will and perfect will," "saved but not secure," "certain but elusive." These and countless similar phrases are contrived by those who have not found the place of accepting God's love as totally inclusive and His power as strong enough to accomplish His will in their lives and in the lives of those around them.

I have discovered unconditional love in the Love Shack. This is my personal place of refuge, hope, and confidence.

Just as our conversations with the ones we love change as we experience love, so our conversation with our Lord changes as we find assurance in His Presence. My prayers have changed significantly over the years. I am no longer the uncertain beggar trying to convince God of my worthiness to be blessed. I do not try to convince Him I am worthy to love. I am not. I know it, He knows it, and He laughs, for His love is "just because." He loves—no explanation needed. He loves, period. If there is any convincing to be done, it is in my need to accept His incredible unconditional love for me.

Oh, I know that we are taught about His unconditional love, but religion always seems to give it conditions. What? How can unconditional love have conditions? This is just one of religion's many outrageous oxymorons. Conditional unconditional love is a conundrum that will never find its way into the resting place of the Love Shack, for it opposes everything for which Jesus gave Himself.

No Advice for God

I no longer counsel the Lord in my prayers. I have ceased to clutter the spiritual air with personal opinions and directives. He has convinced me that I can trust Him. He has convinced me that He always has my best interest at heart. My prayer times have changed from the beggar to the lover. Now my conversations with Him are much like the conversations I have with my wife. Cathy and I know that we can trust each other. I don't have to worry or wonder about her fulfilling her daily responsibilities any more than she has to worry about me fulfilling mine. We do not remind each other of the so-called mundane things of everyday life that we do in response to our love for each other. Love constrains us to do things we have promised or know that we must do. Duties are a joy because we are pleasing the one we love and, for the most part, are not considered duties but rather true expressions of love for each other.

Now if this be true in a human relationship, how much more is it true in relationship to our Lord Jesus?

Christ's love controls us... (2 Corinthians 5:14).

I have ceased to clutter the spiritual air with personal opinions and directives.

God's love is manifest to us in all He does and is to us. He does not need to be reminded about anything, any more than Cathy needs to remind me to take out the garbage or I need to remind her to buy groceries. Love joyfully compels us to serve each other.

When we are together, we are enjoying each other's company and we talk about things that reinforce and complement our love for each other. Everything we do we do with each other in mind. We rest in the knowledge that experienced love builds faith and rest in each other's love. It is a remarkable experience, indeed.

I often pray, "Lord, don't give us more faith; give us more love." Faith will then follow as a natural consequence of that love.

WHAT PEOPLE WANT — WHAT PEOPLE NEED

People want to be loved, redeemed, restored, sent, fulfilled, and happy. But all these words can be wrapped into one: destiny.

And destiny finds its fulfillment in relationship. I do not mean the typical definition of a relationship with God. You know the one I am talking about—a relationship with God as a three-minute prayer that assures your ticket to Heaven. That kind of prayer of repentance will certainly bring you to your salvation, but it should not be mistaken for a vibrant one-on-one relationship with your Lord that is meaningful, fulfilling, possible, and greatly desired by Him.

Are you truly looking for both truth and a personal experience?

If you can deliver any of this message in a book with compassion, mercy, and hope, you will sell books. If there is one thing I have learned during my 25 years of Christian publishing, it is this: a book that accurately portrays the purposes of God will find its way to those who need it. The converse, however, is not true. There are many, many, *many* books that sell simply because they feed the fleshly appetites of carnal Christianity. Those books will always be best-sellers, but will never satisfy our inner needs of friendship with God and the sense of eternal purpose that we all covet. But there is also a third type of Christian book—one that gives you all the things you want and promises everything, but at the end of the day, delivers little. This is the most sinister, for it masquerades as a book of fulfillment but delivers only a hope for the afterlife, while leaving you alone in the here and now to struggle your way through life.

Are you truly looking for both truth *and* a personal experience? Are you interested in merely believing in something intellectual, or do you want what you believe in to become active in your life? If the latter, you are the one I am writing to. You are the one who is content only with the complete work of the Cross in your heart and life. You want to experience the Kingdom of God now, while you are alive to enjoy its glory, power, and relationship.

The good news: God wants this for you too. It is what He intended in eternity past when He had you on His heart and could hardly wait for the time of your appearance on this planet.

More than anything else, God wants His dreams for you to come to pass.

More than anything else, God wants His dreams for you to come to pass. After all, that is why Jesus came to earth in the first place. His redemption goes far beyond our pitiful abilities to describe the wonders of multidimensional living and the eternity in which these dimensions exist. When you were conceived within your mother's womb and then burst onto the scene both in time and space and in eternity, your spirit was (and continues to be) fresh and alive as you instantly began to discover, process, and learn about God's creation. When you were born, the world made room for you, knowing that almighty God had destined your arrival and knowing that God had designed a plan that He fully intended for you to fulfill. The heavens are at your disposal, ready to help in every way to accomplish God's dream for your existence.

And so they are—the heavens are ready to work on your behalf far more radically than you can possibly imagine, far more aggressively than you can hope, and with far more attentiveness than you are used to giving. The Love Shack is the destination of relationship, out of which fulfillment blossoms.

HIS ANGELS

In my book *Romancing the Divine*, I describe an encounter that expresses His infinite love for us. The experience follows:

> The morning chill made me shiver as I awoke on the riverbank. A pale mist rose from the water as the sun shot its first rays through the trees of this unknown woodland. I could see birds flying from tree to tree, but their songs were drowned by the rushing of the river. Angels guarded the clearing. A fire burned close by. The crackling of the fire and the warmth of its flames offered a pleasant and reassuring reminder of the night before and the peace the Lord had brought to my heart. An angel served me hot tea and warm bread, thus completing this idyllic morning.
>
> I had not seen Him since He rode off several hours earlier, but somehow, I knew He was near.

The memory of the night before was so sweet. Some folks may have wondered if it was all just a dream, or maybe just the work of an overactive imagination. I knew better. This was not my imagination.

I had been a believer for many years. I thought I knew the power of His love. But last night was remarkable. I could never deny it; nor could anyone explain it away. I knew what I had experienced; I knew what I saw, what I heard, what I touched. No one could take that away from me. I had passed from death into life, from despair into hope, from guilt into freedom.

He said that His burden was easy and His load light, I thought. But this is wonderful, far more than I could ever have expected. I am afraid I gloated in my newfound sense of acceptance and love from the Lord. Now this, this is born again!

As I thought about these heart issues, I began to feel a new joy and power welling up from within. I laughed as I watched the angels in this small clearing. How real this realm of eternity is! How silly are our human efforts to deny its awesome power and existence. I felt the restraints dropping from my mind and spirit. After so many years, I had finally touched the eternity of God, for I touched God.

It really is funny, you know. So much time is spent trying to explain away the reality of this dimension that is infinitely more powerful than the one we live in. It is no wonder to me that no human words, no human doctrines or intellectual dissertations, no frightened and insecure people can talk away what has been from eternity past and will exist to eternity future. Humanity does not possess the vocabulary to snuff out the fire of His life that burns with such consuming brilliance in the hearts of His people worldwide.

How ironic. We argue creationism to the secular world, but we deny the power of the dimension we so vehemently believe created the world and all it contains.

So here I sat, watching angels, so real, so tangible, so protective. I had peace that I had not experienced in years; I had freedom from guilt, freedom from heavy burdens...I felt as though I could fly, I was so light. Who would not want this salvation, this forgiveness for this life as well as the next?

"Jesus, if this is what Your Kingdom brings, then absolutely I will pray with You, 'Thy kingdom come, Thy will be done, on earth as it is in heaven.' Absolutely, Lord. This is what I want. My loyalty is to You, the only One who can accomplish this in the earth; the only One who can build the Church; the only One whose burden is light and marvelous and enticing and beautiful and glorious and eternal. You have my heart. You really do."

The sun shone through the trees as I prayed.

The wind gently blew over me, carrying the scent of what seemed to be honeysuckle.[1]

It is time to discover your personal Love Shack.

Chapter 3

THE LOVE SHACK MEANS LOVE FOREVER

The reality of what was accomplished by Jesus on the Cross is our assurance that the work of the Lord is based in a deep and eternal love that cannot be understood by the natural mind. In our humanness we want to put our feelings onto the Lord. We want to give Him our prejudices and our limitations. We build walls around our denominations and place heavy burdens on the people of God. We put such burden on believers that their lives are preoccupied with trying to stay saved and trying to toe the company line rather than fulfilling their God-given destinies.

It is no wonder that these words from *The Shack* resonate so loudly in the hearts of those who diligently search for the reality and tangibleness of His love.

> He realized he was stuck, and Sunday prayers and hymns weren't cutting it anymore, if they ever really had. Cloistered spirituality seemed to change

49

nothing in the lives of the people he knew, except maybe Nan. But she was special. God might really love her. She wasn't a screw-up like him. He was sick of God and God's religion, sick of all the little religious social clubs that didn't seem to make any real difference or affect any real changes.[1]

God is *not* like us! That is precisely why He is God. Our judgments are based on exasperation rather than mercy, and we execute condemnation that is based on the stinging letter of the unyielding Law rather than the overwhelming power of His limitless grace.

> *You hate My discipline (instruction). You turn your back on what I say. When you see a thief, you want to join him. You take part in adultery. You do not stop your mouth from speaking evil. Your tongue makes up lies. You sit there speaking against your brother. You slander your mother's son. I have kept quiet while you did these things. I will accuse you (make a case) to your face* (Psalm 50:17-21).

Of course, we are not free to sin, but on the other hand, we do not live with such a fickle God that He turns His back on us every time we fail. We were bought with a price. He knows we are but grass. He made us that way so we would live close to Him, circumspectly walking before God in truth, even if the truth shows us to be short of His glory. We are not afraid to admit our shortcomings in the Presence of an all-merciful, all-forgiving God. His mercy is lavishly poured upon us, and His grace is sufficient. We can confidently go to Him in repentance, knowing we are forgiven even before we ask Him. It is simple—we fail, we repent, we go forward. We never lose our step. We need to trust our salvation to Him and go do the will of God.

WHAT HAPPENED WHEN JESUS ASCENDED INTO HEAVEN?

I love to imagine what happens in the dimension of Spirit. It opens my mind to actually experience that dimension as I am not so prone to so quickly dismiss what reality is opened to me. It also helps me to understand the reality of God the Father and His Son, Jesus. These happenings lead us directly to the Love Shack, the place of His abiding Presence. It helps to see that Father, Son, and all spiritual beings experience emotion, thought, pain, and joy. They are as alive as we are, except in a dimension that cannot be perceived by the five senses. In the dimension of eternity, their reality is much greater than what we experience on this side.

Considering the power and awe of this dimension of spirit is why the church system, and religion in general, is only an extremely feeble representation of the reality that is Him. He is constantly urging us to relinquish that which is shadow so we can embrace and experience what is spiritual and will live forever.

The Shack puts the perspective right where it belongs, in the heart, where real relationships grow and flourish with joy unspeakable!

"I don't create institutions—never have, never will," Jesus said.

"What about the institution of marriage?"

"Marriage is not an institution. It's a relationship." Jesus paused, his voice steady and patient. "Like I said, I don't create institutions; that's an occupation for those who want to play God. So no, I'm not too big on religion," Jesus said a little sarcastically....[2]

LOVE THAT TRANSCENDS ETERNITY

As you read the following account of Jesus ascending into the Presence of His Father, remember that the Father sees you in exactly the same way that He sees His firstborn Son, Jesus. His love for you is undying and His grace unending. You are not strong enough to pull yourself away from Him. Did you get that? I know this is much different from what you are used to hearing. I know it is not what you expected to read, but it is true. You are not stronger than the blood that redeemed you or the love that holds you.

You are not stronger than the blood that redeemed you or the love that holds you.

You should be and are intended to be certain of His love and the redeeming power of His love to hold, forgive, and restore you. You need to spend your time, energy, anointing, and creativity fulfilling His dreams for you, not trying to simply stay saved. If you have the power to keep yourself saved, then you could have saved yourself without the blood of Jesus.

Your heavenly Father welcomes you into His Presence as He welcomed His Son, Jesus. The following is how it might have happened. I wrote this a few years ago to help others understand the reality of the dimensions we do not see with our five senses and the incredible true love relationship that did exist and continues to exist between Father God and His Son, Jesus. Put yourself in Christ's place as you read this account from my book *Romancing the Divine.*

> As I watched the Lord walk toward the torn veil holding a cup of His own blood, there was every confidence, every anticipation of a joyous, rollicking reunion. He turned toward me, "Come closer, watch what will happen."
>
> He turned back toward the curtain, and holding the cup of His own blood in His right hand, He slowly pulled open the torn veil with His left hand and walked in. The moment the curtain opened, the glorious, blinding lights of His Presence exploded from the Most Holy Place. I instinctively covered my face with my arms.
>
> "Wow!" was all I could say. The Light swirled round and round, filling every crevice of the Holy Place, and then streamed through to the Outer Court and beyond.
>
> *The Light seems to have a mind of its own. It seems to be alive,* I thought. It raced to the horizon and expanded without losing even a bit of its brilliance.

As much as I wanted to follow this unfolding drama, I turned my attention to inside the veil. This was an event I did not want to miss.

The moment the curtain opened, the glorious, blinding lights of His Presence exploded from the Most Holy Place.

I opened the veil ever so slightly to look in. I again shielded my eyes from the intensity of the glory within. I slowly uncovered them, hoping they would get used to the brilliance of the light. But I could not manage much more than just pale outlines in the blinding glow of His manifest Presence.

I saw enough to be transfixed by what was happening. The Son walked slowly, reverently, confidently. He was glowing with a translucent radiance of another dimension. He existed in two places at one time. He was in the Presence of the Father, but He was enough on this side for me to follow Him. The closer He walked, the brighter the pulsating light of His manifest Presence responded. The cherubim on either side of the Presence fidgeted slightly in anticipation of the approach of the Son. He walked within inches of the Presence.

I was no longer in the temple laid with types

and shadows of what is in Heaven. I was *there*. The real cherubim glowed with exponential brilliance over the golden statues of the temple. The Mercy Seat, overlaid with gold, was the throne of the Ancient of Days, whose nature and character is mercy. And there He sat, covered with unapproachable light—light so powerful, so penetrating, so all-seeing, that mere unprotected flesh cannot survive in His Presence.

"Father," I heard Him speak softly, lovingly.

"Here it is."

He looked down at the earthenware bottle in His hand. His fresh wounds were visible as He extended His arm toward His Father.

"Here is the cup of My blood."

I could barely make out His form in the brightness of His Father's glory. With His arm still outstretched, He took another step toward the throne of God, the Seat of Mercy, preparing to give the cup to His Father.

"This is for You, Father. I did it for You, just as You asked Me to."

He lifted the cup with both hands and presented it to His Father. The angels could barely contain their suspense. They moved more noticeably now, as the Son continued to speak.

"I love You, My Father. This cup, with all it contains, with all it has accomplished, is Yours."

There was a deep groan from the very depth, the very heart of the Light, as Father stood to His feet. Through the brilliance of His splendor, I could barely make out the pale silhouettes of Father and Son falling toward each other, grasping one another with an embrace that no words can describe.

The cup of blood fell from His hand, splattering both Father and Son with blood that ever liveth.

The cup of blood fell from His hand, splattering both Father and Son with blood that ever liveth. The force of their embrace knocked the cup directly onto the throne, the ultimate Mercy Seat, as Father pulled His Son forward to Himself, still locked in loving embrace.

"Sit here, O Son of My love. Sit here with Me, right next to Me." Songs of triumph and victory filled Heaven as the angels sang the songs only they could sing, in languages only they could understand.

"What You have done, You have done once and for all time. You will never leave My Presence again. Come, sit here with Me, forever."

The falling cup shattered against the Mercy Seat, sending the blood in every direction. It covered the Mercy Seat and the poles that lay at its feet in this dimension, and the blood covered the throne in the dimension of eternity. It splattered against its badger-skin walls and fell to the ground in front of the torn veil in this dimension, to just in front of the Mercy Seat.

The splattered blood made an eternal pathway from the place of my humanity to His Presence. It splashed onto the cherubim that stood guard, sending them into a crescendo of worship that opened the heavens and invited a myriad of angels to sing the ultimate intention of the Lord: "The kingdoms of this world have become the kingdoms of our Lord and of His Christ!"

Then nature itself responded. From the distant mountains, somewhere between eternity and time, came a rumbling, a clapping like the most awful thunderbolt ever heard, and a rift between dimensions opened in glorious splendor. Instantly, blackened clouds rolled down the mountainside as though hungrily looking for prey. Lightning opened the sky as Heaven was split open from side to side. Another rampaging, thunderous roar exploded from the mountain, and the voice of God Himself could be heard pouring from eternity, proclaiming from one side of the universe to another, "I, Myself, have brought My deliverance. My right hand, and My holy arm have gotten for Me the victory!"

His thundering words blazed through eternity, breaking into time and space, in and out and through every epoch of every time the earth had or will experience, vaporizing every obstacle as though it were less than nothing. His words searched out every darkness and every evil. They ravaged every sickness and destroyed every bondage. His voice crushed every lie and shattered every tormenting word spewed from the mouth of hell. It pulverized every lofty human arrogance and finally swallowed up death itself.

His words searched out every darkness and every evil. They ravaged every sickness and destroyed every bondage.

Then His words spewed satan's awful intention into the lake of fire that will burn forever and ever. "The cup of My blood! The cup of My blood!" the sweet voice of the Son echoed through the ages and into Heaven as His Father gathered His only Begotten forever to Himself, nevermore to be separated.

"This cup is for You, Father!" But Father barely heard the words as He declared to the universe, "My Beloved Son, My Beloved Son!"

Then with a crack of a mighty timber, the gates of hell tore open, and the redeemed of the Lord shouted with joyous clamor. Union with God had been accomplished!

And then I looked, and the heavens opened, as the shattering of the cup had splintered the division between Heaven and earth, between where we had lived and where He has prepared us to live with Him. Then I heard the voice of many angels around the throne and the living creatures and the elders, and the number of them was myriads of myriads, and thousands of thousands, saying with a loud voice: "Worthy is the Lamb who was slain to receive power and riches and wisdom and might and honor and glory and blessing."

And Heaven and earth united in a moment that transcended eternity. The groaning of the earth, of things created on our side, joined with every living thing on the other side. The sound of that from Heaven could not be distinguished from the sound of that which arose from every created thing on earth. I could never have imagined anything like it, as everything that is in Heaven and on the earth and under the earth and on the sea, and all things in them, cried out with deafening worship, "To Him who sits on the throne, and to the Lamb, be blessing and honor and glory and dominion forever and ever."

And still other angels appeared from the heavens, shouting, "Worthy are You to take the book, and to break its seals; for You were slain and did purchase for God with Your blood men from every tribe and tongue and people and nation. And You have made them to be a kingdom and priests to our God, and they will reign upon the earth."

Then I saw the Lord seated in union with His Father upon the Mercy Seat. His form was now clearly visible as the hosts of Heaven continued to worship, sing, shout, dance, and worship.

"Yes!" I shouted with the angels. "It is finished! It truly is finished!"

> *The Father Himself, with hilarious joy, calls to humanity, "Come on in! Take a seat and watch Me make your enemies a hassock for your feet!"*

I was overwhelmed with the wonder of all that was happening in this realm of eternity. I was shocked at the reality of such joyful confidence and complete commitment the Lord has toward us. Oh, how foolish the guilt! How foolish the fear! How foolish the time I have wasted, the things I have believed! I am loved! I am loved!

His blood calls to humanity, "Come on in!" The Son calls to humanity, "Come on in! I have prepared a seat for you next to your Father and Mine, your God and Mine." The Father Himself, with hilarious joy, calls to humanity, "Come on in!

Take a seat and watch Me make your enemies a hassock for your feet!"

Nonetheless, I was happy to be peeking through the veil from the Holy Place, hiding as best I could from this supernatural opus of total rapture toward the One who sits on the throne. As much as I wanted to be part of this, dare I believe? Could He have been referring to me as well? Dare I go in knowing what I know about myself, with all that still troubles me?

The Lord saw me looking through the veil and motioned for me to come in. It was quite unbelievable that He would even notice me in the midst of such deafening worship.

But I wondered, *Dare I believe?*

The blood splattered on the floor glistened as brightly as the light that pulsated from between the cherubim. Could it be? Was He calling out to me? It did not take long for everything inside of me to cry out to Him. I wanted to run to Him. Almost against my will I inched ever so slowly through the veil.

"This is just a dream or vision," I tried to reassure myself. "I have already been through this." But I am afraid I was not too convincing. Without warning I let go of the veil. There I stood, just inside the Most Holy Place, where He is Lord, where His will supersedes my will, where I relinquish my arguments and trust Him. But I was overcome with the knowledge that He had prepared a place for me as well on the very Seat where He sat with His Father.

In the splendor of that wonderful moment, all my fears and my meager human frailty seemed to be nothing against the power of the love of the Lord calling me to Himself. I was about to run to Him. My flesh screamed as it began to realize it was about to lose its favored position as counselor and confidant of all my decisions.

Then I finally did it. I dropped everything I could and ran for all I was worth. Yes, I tripped over my own personal clutter. I clanged with all the fleshly stuff still tightly fastened to me. I knew I was in desperate need; I knew I looked rather unkempt to myself, but I also knew He was calling me. I ran to Him, to His open arms, to His open heart, to His mercy, and to His forgiveness. I ran to His power to deliver and His desire for the likes of someone like me. I ran to His smiling face that seemed to hold as much anticipation as a mother watching her child take his first steps.

The clutter and clang of all I still dragged with me was drowned by the glory of angelic worship. The blinding light of His manifest Presence made my humanity disappear as I approached Him who dwells in unapproachable Light. In a moment I was with Him or in Him or beside Him, in this dimension or the other, I did not know and I did not really care what correct doctrinal spin to give it. I knew I was in my body, but I also knew I was in Him, really in Him. Oh, but it did not matter if I could explain it. I would leave that part to those who try to figure out events like this. I would simply enjoy Him. All I did know for sure was that I was completely consumed by Him.

The clutter and clang of all I still dragged with me was drowned by the glory of angelic worship.

"My yoke is easy," He whispered to me, "and My burden is light." I held Him and I held Him and I held Him.

"Let My Blood cover you until My power delivers you." He held me and He held me and He held me.

"I will put all your enemies exactly where they belong," the Lord spoke with eternal resolve, "right under your feet."

I found myself whispering softly to Him as He gathered me to Himself, "Yes, yes, yes, Lord. Thy Kingdom come. Thy will be done on earth as it is in Heaven. Thy Kingdom come in me, in my heart. Thy will be done in me, on earth, exactly as

You have dreamed it for me in Heaven. Yes, yes, Lord. Yes, Lord."[3]

What a glorious experience this was for me. This description gives fresh meaning to the Scripture, "We are seated with Him in heavenly places in Christ Jesus" (see Eph. 2:6). The reality of the spirit realm and of our place with Him is most important to understand. We are not involved in a fairy tale. There is a multidimensional reality that we have not yet grasped. There is a participation in all things divine that we have not yet touched. These incredible truths are awaiting our involvement right now, while we still breathe, for He has chosen us before the foundations of the earth for this daily experience.

And God raised us from spiritual death and seated us in the heavenly world with Christ Jesus (Ephesians 2:6).

Although life is a journey, that does not mean we never end up where we want to go. For years we have been taught that we will never get to Him or reach our goals. Our lives are only spent *chasing* what we desire and love. But this is absolutely contrary to what happened when Jesus rose from the dead, and this hopeless teaching of running but never arriving opposes everything that Jesus wants for us. There is an arrival in this life. There is a rest in this life. There is a fellowship in this life. In fact, the reality of

Kingdom life here and now was so real to the early church that Paul had to remind the believers that there was more to salvation than just this life. "If we have put our hope in Christ in this life, and Christ did not rise from death, then, of all people, we should be pitied the most" (1 Cor. 15:19).

Our inner yearning for fulfillment is intended to be satisfied in this life. Marriage would not be complete if there were not true fulfillment emotionally, physically, and spiritually. There are many adventures that marriage takes us on, but we know the adventure is the result of the fulfillment, not the search for it. The marriage relationship is the fulfillment we want. If we do not have fulfillment in the relationship, then no adventure, no matter how exciting it may be, will bring contentment into the marriage.

Likewise, our journey to the Love Shack is the beginning of a lifetime of fellowship with our Lord. Instead of a lifetime of searching for the fellowship and intimacy of the Love Shack, He has intended a lifetime of fulfillment and fellowship with Him in the Love Shack.

WHAT IS SPIRITUAL INTIMACY?

You may have discovered that the things of the natural are opposite of the things of the spirit. For instance, in the spiritual realm, to be first you have to be last. To lead, you must be servant of all. To be mature, you have to become like a child. To receive, you have to give.

Intimacy is another one of those words that does not mean what we have supposed it to mean. The true definition of intimacy must be understood from a spiritual perspective. It is difficult to find words to adequately explain the interaction between humankind and God. It involves processes that have no human words to describe. I am convinced that Paul struggled with this concept when he wrote:

He has intended a lifetime of fulfillment and fellowship with Him in the Love Shack.

It is not the spirit of the world which we have received. Instead, we received the Spirit who comes from God, so that we may understand the things which God gave to us. These are the things we are saying. We are not using human ideas of wisdom which man taught us. Instead, we are using words which the Spirit teaches. We explain Spiritual things with Spiritual words (1 Corinthians 2:12-13).

How do we describe this interweaving of God and humankind? How do we express the sense of lovely submission to His Spirit as He fills, possesses, and consumes mere human beings with His wondrous Presence?

Remember that Jesus is within us. He wants to live His divine life through us. He wants to display His personality (the fruit of the Spirit) and His power (the gifts of the Spirit) through us. Therefore, intimacy is an intricate union of His will and our hearts.

It is a blending of Him into our personality, our heart, and our desires so that He shines perfectly through us in all we do.

> *My little children, again I feel pain for you, such*
> *as a mother feels when she gives birth to her child.*
> *I will feel this, until Christ is fully formed in you*
> (Galatians 4:19).

This coming together of His Person in us is true intimacy.

Intimacy is the holy trust between us and our Lord that allows us to shed our fleshly selves, exposing our nakedness before Him, that He may clothe us with Himself, His unapproachable Light that convinces the world that Jesus is Lord. We always thought it was our dress, our words, our preaching, or our religious demeanor that showed the world that Jesus was Lord. In fact, it is those things that make the world wonder if He really is Lord. He wants to shine through our personality, much like the brilliant sun shining through a stained glass window. The window is beautiful in itself, but with the sun shining through it, the stained glass comes alive.

When we yield our lives to Him that He may shine through us, we become alive in Him. Our mere presence convinces the world that God is alive and well on this planet. This coming together of His Person in us is true intimacy. It is a union as holy and private as the marriage bed, for it is in this union that we truly take on the divine nature, shedding the clothing of works and man-made religion.

Let's go back to *Romancing the Divine*. In this next segment, we can begin to understand, if only a tiny bit, the magnitude of the work of Jesus and His plan for us to be in Him and He in us.

> I sat there on the Mercy Seat for the longest time, enjoying His Presence, but sorry that this was only a vision of what had already occurred in eternity. I knew that any moment He would awaken me or do whatever it was He did to take us back to where we had begun this side trip. The Lord had used these wonderful adventures to teach me some of the most incredible things, but this was truly the most incredible of them all.
>
> "Thank You, Lord," I ventured to say to Him. "This is so overwhelming, so wonderful."
>
> I hesitated to tell Him how I felt, but I had new confidence to talk to Him as the true Friend that He had become. "I do not want to go back," I said rather sheepishly, "but I guess we have to."
>
> The Lord turned to me with an inquisitive look. "Why would you want to go back? If I were you, I would want to stay right here."
>
> "Well, I do want to stay here, Lord. But I thought we always returned from these adventures once You had taught me everything I needed to see." My words drifted into silence with the realization

that He had somehow brought my reality into His reality. Somehow, dimension had converged upon dimension and this was reality. This was not just a side trip. I actually was here in the midst of all the worshiping angelic hosts and in the Presence of the Father Himself!

"Lord, how did this happen?" I stammered. "I do not understand." I stood to look around the throne. "I do not remember seeing all this within the veil. I do not remember seeing or hearing the angels. The cherubim were gold statues—now they are real. The Mercy Seat had only a light on it, and now the Father sits there. It was so quiet before, just You and I sitting there on the Mercy Seat. Now I can see and hear all this wonderful heavenly activity."

The Lord smiled gently, as usual. "Yes, we were on the Mercy Seat, but this side trip opened your spiritual eyes to see things that you could not see before. Everything you see here now is as it was before. Now, however, you have eyes to see so much more of the things that were here all along. And there is much more for you to see and experience beyond the veil, beyond your fleshly self with all its demands and earthbound requirements.

"Life will never be the same. I will teach you things you thought you knew and show you things you were sure you understood. In many ways, your life will be turned upside down, or, more accurately, right side up. For as the doctrines and traditions of men are challenged by truth, you will discover the true freedom of Christ and understand the bondage you had been under for so many years."

"Life will never be the same."

I could not help but be a bit uncertain as I heard these words. "But, Lord," I began, "people are always afraid of talk like that. They are not sure what they will get into if they hear the voice of the Lord for themselves. I have heard of some pretty strange things they claim You have said to them. Some say You are from Mars; some hear stones talking to them; some expect to see their dogs in Heaven."

"Yes, yes," the Lord stopped me with a smile, "I have some stories too."

"I bet You do," I returned the smile. "I guess that is why they say you can never count on your own interpretation of Scripture in your search for truth."

"That is easy to understand," the Lord countered. "They really are not so concerned about error. They do not want you to listen for yourself because they just want you to believe *their* interpretation of the Scripture. Some do not trust the Holy Spirit to lead their flocks into truth, so they attempt to prohibit them from listening to Me."

"But people do get into some awfully weird things in the name of Christianity," I protested to the Lord. I couldn't believe I was defending these people.

"It is true that people get into things that are far from accurate. But how does that justify preventing the free, uninhibited seeking in all the divine wonder and glory? Just because some miss the mark, should the entire Church be punished? If the truth really be told, people still end up in error even with so many restrictions in place."

"But Lord, I want to be certain that everything I hear and everything I do is absolutely scriptural, absolutely accurate."

"That is a noble statement, truly an admirable goal. But if you are so committed to that goal, why do you entrust your future to someone else? Why do you entrust your knowledge of the Lord and your love relationship to Him to anyone but the Lover of your soul? Look, I am totally trustworthy. You can trust what I say. I do not violate My own Word," the Lord said with resolution. "Everything I say, everything I do, is according to the Word. You must remember, I AM the Word. The actual writing of it was an attempt to describe the nearly indescribable. I cannot do anything that will violate Myself and who I represent."

I already knew that, but somehow it was reassuring to hear that from Him. Still, there seemed to be something more He was not telling me, so I just waited. He finally turned to me with a twinkle in His eyes. "However...," He began.

I knew it! There was more, and I was about to hear it.

"However," the Lord began again, "although I can never violate My Word, I will [often] violate what men think My Word says."

"However," the Lord began again, "although I can never violate My Word, I will [often] violate what men think My Word says. There is a big difference." Here the Lord paused with a smile. He shook His head and continued, "Man will create doctrine out of the genuine conviction that he has properly understood and interpreted the Word. But when someone disagrees with that determined truth, that person is accused of heresy. Even more perplexing is when I do something that violates doctrine. How quick they are to attribute My work to the flesh or satan! It is as though protecting their belief system is more important than the reality of My Presence.

"You must remember, although many want to experience God, that experience will not often fit within the context of what you have always believed. Your experience is not with a doctrine—it is with a Person.

"It is the sheer arrogance of humanity that believes that humans have unraveled the mysteries of an eternal God and the complexities of His infinite love and mercies. We have existed from eternity past and We will exist for eternity future. Far after time has ceased, We will still be as though We have just begun. Mere mortals believe that they have so understood My majesty and My multidimensional Being that they can judge others' salvation using their own textbooks as a plumb line. These folks search the Scriptures for truth, and they miss Me as they would rather intricately examine the robe upon My back."

I just shook my head in wonder. "I do not remember all this in the Book," I said to myself. "I learned what is right and wrong by reading the Book, but never all of this."

As I spoke, the Lord pulled out the Book. It was small, and the deep burgundy leather cover was slightly tattered. The pages were frayed slightly on the edges, and the black ribbon to mark the page was seriously worn. This Book looked familiar, like the one on the nightstand next to my bed.

"You have been reading this for years."

"Yes, I have, Lord."

"But it brought you more frustration than peace."

I was so embarrassed, but He was right. "Yes, Lord, it has brought me a fair amount of frustration."

"Do you understand why it so unsettled you as you read?"

"Well, I guess it was because I could never do what it said for me to do. It was so difficult to read sometimes."

"Ah," He interrupted me. "That is the problem. It is always the problem."

"Reading the Book is a problem?"

"Reading the Book is not a problem. Reading it alone with only the five senses to help you understand is a big, big problem." He opened the Book randomly as He spoke. Then He held it up high over His head.

"Look, tell Me what you see."

"Look where?"

"Look into the Book."

"I cannot read it when You hold it up like that."

"Just look up into the Book."

I moved closer to the Lord so I could see more clearly. I could feel His warmth as I nudged closer. *Wow,* I thought, *this is quite a perk. I get to be closer to Him as I read.*

Then I lifted my head and peered into the

Book. I wondered what was on the page that was so important. I had thought that He opened the Book randomly. I squinted as I looked, assuming that He wanted me to read something special there. I held my breath in amazement as I discovered what the Lord wanted me to see.

It was not a book at all—it was a window through which the most indescribable things could be seen.

As I looked up at the Book with Him holding it, I realized that I was not looking at the Book, I was looking *through* the Book. In fact, it was not a book at all. It was a window through which the most indescribable things could be seen.

"Lord, what is this? I thought this was my copy of the Book, but this is some kind of special...."

"There is nothing special about this Book, except that I am holding it and directing your view."

"You mean all this is not really here? It is not real?"

"Oh, it is certainly real enough, but it is not visible in the natural dimension. It is not detectable by the five senses."

"Oh, my Lord, this is unbelievable. This is so awesome! How did You do this?"

"When you read with Me close, I direct the eyes of your spirit and lift your heart to a place of revelation and wisdom."

"But this is my Book. I have never seen any of this before."

"It is there when you want to see it."

As I gazed through this open window, I saw the wonders of eternity itself. I saw His love intricately woven through everything that lived. His Life grew out of every word that proceeded from His mouth. His Spirit flowed from His heart to the hearts of uncountable millions. His mercy and grace sang "Come" and His blood covered everyone who called upon Him as they ventured nearer to His throne. He reached out His hand, inscribing His laws forever on willing and hungry hearts while all the angels sang of His power and fell prostrate before Him. His joy bubbled from the lives of children and adults alike as darkness and crying fled at the sound of His voice.

"This is beyond description." I shook my head in stunned disbelief. "How does one talk about this?" I asked the Lord.

"You don't, mostly." The Lord responded with quiet joy, His eyes shining with satisfaction to see how I had responded to the wonders of His Kingdom.

"This is not something that can be understood

by the senses in the natural dimension. This must be experienced spirit to Spirit."

I am sorry to say that I did not quite get it, so He went on.

"The written Word is not a textbook. It is not a list of what is necessary to reserve a place in Heaven. It is not a neatly defined protocol of religious activity. The Word is a window through which you may see and understand the dimension of the eternal. It is how you are able to discover the boundless wonder and mystery of an eternal God who is far bigger and far more majestic than humankind can comprehend."[4]

The Word is a window through which you may see and understand the dimension of the eternal.

YOUR PERSONAL LOVE SHACK EXPERIENCE

There is no way to describe what your experience will be. But I am certain that your life with Jesus in the Love Shack will be full of joy, love, wholeness, and revelation. It is a place of comfort, compassion, mercy, and grace. It is a place where you see the world around you as He sees it. As a result, you begin to think as He thinks, love as He loves, and give as He gives, for who He is pours out of Him and into you. Soon, you will not be able to distinguish your thoughts from His, your love from His, your compassion from His. Your mind will change. You will realize that you are being transformed as your mind is being melded with His. This is truly a most holy place. Union with Him will change everything about you. He will change you from a mere mortal to His child. You will be on a new adventure that will take a glorious and exciting lifetime to experience!

Within the Love Shack is the portal to all that is eternal, all that is divine, all that is Him. You will enjoy a lifetime of wonder and discovery as He is in you and you are in Him. It is what He purchased for you. It is what He intends for you.

Chapter 4

THE LOVE SHACK MEANS WHOLENESS

Contrary to popular belief, it is not the intention of the Lord for us to spend our lifetime in personal introspection and analysis. Those who spend time probing the inner sanctums of their existence can easily become lost in the myriad of human complexities that we have no business dabbling in. Our minds are like unexplored caverns. We should not be spending time spelunking in caves that hide who knows what.

Our focus must remain on Him and His destiny for us, with the full expectation that He will do the inner probing and changing that is required. He knows what lurks within us and He has the expertise to set us free. I suggest we serve Him and wait for Him to do the hunting. He is always on time, knowing just when to pull that old black bear out and deal with him!

HIS WORK, YOUR WORK

When Peter went fishing after denying Jesus three times, our

Lord found him on the seaside and encouraged him in his grief. Peter had denied his Lord and could not face himself or his Lord in this failure. Peter had finally come face to face with himself in his weakness and humanity. Jesus simply told him to go do the will of God. "Be a shepherd to My sheep" (John 21:16). Jesus responded to Peter's personal discovery of his own inadequacy. Jesus assured Peter that one day he would be strong enough to die for Him. Jesus knew that as Peter concentrated on doing the will of God, the Lord would center on the reconstruction, maintenance, and wholeness that Peter saw he was lacking but so desperately wanted. Jesus would work in Peter's life in a way that would allow Peter to continue his work in the Kingdom of God, without distracting him or discouraging him to the point where he would not be an effective disciple. In essence, Jesus said to Peter, "My ministry is to change you. Your ministry is to change the world. You do your work and I will do Mine."

Life within the Love Shack is a wonderful experience of Spirit and Truth.

Times of introspection will come as you allow the Lord to show you aspects of your life that need His teaching and correction. This will undoubtedly give you a new way to live. Divine instructions are never unto death, but unto repentance and change. In my book *Tales of Brokenness*, this is shown as a powerful way to live. The believer simply concentrates on doing the will of God, while the Holy Spirit quietly and gently transforms us from the inside out.

These two processes begin independently, but converge as time goes on. Your life will reflect His life, and your words become more His words as He teaches you and you find yourself yielding to the instruction He gives deep within your heart. It is an amazing thing. You realize that you do not have to act like Jesus, for acting like Jesus is the result of *not* yielding to Him so He can live His own life through you. Acting is the practice of those who do not submit to His life within.

Life within the Love Shack is a wonderful experience of Spirit and Truth as you yield to the sound of His voice. In the next few pages, taken from my book *Tales of Brokenness,* you will discover the divine convergence of natural and spiritual, soul and spirit. You will see the result of this heavenly, multidimensional metamorphosis through folks like you and me. It is a humbling, exhilarating process of Christ in you, truly the hope of glory. (See Colossians 1:27.)

BROKENNESS EMBRACED

Quiet reigns in the grassy cove in the cliffs beside the busy road. You are not nearly so tired or discouraged as when you first stopped here to rest with Brokenness. In fact, you feel energy and interest in life you have not known for quite some time. It is as though you have come into the light after groping your way through darkness. And so it is, for the Lord's hand of strength sustains you and

His work in your heart gives you the courage to go on.

Brokenness, sensing that you are ready to resume your journey, stands and turns toward you. "Are you rested now? Shall we go on?"

"Yes, I'm ready to face life again," you respond.

When you rejoin the others on the road, you find yourself once again leaning heavily on Brokenness. You are certain that her nearness is invaluable to you. Where once you hid your sin, now you repent quickly, willingly, and even joyfully. You understand the freedom that confession and repentance bring.

Truly you are experiencing the benefits of friendship with Brokenness. Her nearness keeps the memory of your failures close to your heart. Yet you do not suffer their reproach. In truth, you are wondrously freed from the condemning voices that once filled your mind. It is not that the reality or the memory of your sin is gone, for you are still conscious of how and where you have failed. The wonder of your present life with Brokenness is simply that you no longer judge yourself for what is forgiven and in the past. You are free to love and serve your Lord, repenting when you need to, but still loving and serving Him nonetheless.

This same freedom is also changing how you respond to the shortcomings of others. With the memory of your own failures planted firmly in your mind, you find yourself at an amazing vantage point, one you have never before seen and certainly have never before understood. Something beautiful is happening to you. Your attitudes are changing and your judgments are diminishing. Everything has a new perspective.

Brokenness, hand in hand with her Lord, has done a remarkable thing. Gently leading you close to the heart of God your Father, she has forever changed how you look at the world. Now you see and appreciate the hearts of the people God has put in your life. You understand their struggles and their fears, their dashed dreams and the broken places in their lives. It almost breaks your heart. You never dreamed that they have many of the same joys and sorrows that you do.

With the memory of your own failures planted firmly in your mind, you find yourself at an amazing vantage point, one you have never before seen and certainly have never before understood.

Now you know what others are going through. Now you understand what they are up against. Since you struggle with sin that continually plagues you, you rightly conclude that they also experience persistent struggles. Since your hopes are dashed at times, you assume that they too suffer broken dreams and many frustrations.

"Do you understand what's happening to you?" Brokenness asks. "You are beginning to see through the eyes of your Lord instead of through the selfish eyes of a human being. You are being moved by the needs that move your Father. You are being constrained to respond based on a heart that loves and wants only to serve the Lord by serving the needs of the people around you."

You nod, admitting the truth of her words. For the first time you are seeing humanity as God sees it—struggling to prosper, struggling for happiness, struggling for fulfillment, struggling for love. You also feel His heartache for these men and women He so carefully created, and hear the groan from much deeper in His heart than you can comprehend. His heart is broken. You see His love for you, a yearning for your well-being so great, so intense, that He gave His Son for your redemption, and you understand that even this ultimate sacrifice did not, cannot, relieve the ache of love deep in His heart. Fellowship and communion, intimacy and oneness, only these satisfy Him.

Wonder and awe fill your soul as you finally understand that this same overwhelming love, this same driving passion for union that caused the eternal sacrifice of His Son, is just as strong, just as persistent, and just as unrelenting as it has ever been. *Can it truly be,* you wonder, *that God will not be content until all of us have come to Him and have given ourselves to His love?*

Quickly you turn to Brokenness. Her steady eyes confirm your understanding.

"Not only does God want this union," Brokenness affirms, "but you and all humankind share the need to experience the seemingly elusive yet coveted smile of love and approval from your precious heavenly Father. Your peace of mind, your hopes, and your contentment all hinge on His unconditional love."

Fellowship and communion, intimacy and oneness, only these satisfy Him.

The days ahead reveal the importance of this understanding. You really are changing. Your private place of prayer is fast becoming the most exciting room in your life as God's compassion and love release you to pray freely and decisively for everyone who passes through your life. You marvel that an altered perspective can change your life so much.

Then comes the day when Brokenness brings to mind the one person who wronged you so deeply that you swore—literally—you would never forgive him and certainly never pray for him. "Do you remember what happened one very challenging day when...?" You hesitate, wondering if you can avoid the issue—at least for today. One stern look from Brokenness and you quickly begin to intercede for this person as though your future depends on it. Quite frankly it does, since only a heart free from the torment of unforgiveness can experience and deliver God's love.

Brokenness carefully tends the fruit that is planted in your heart the day you finally forgive and pray for your perceived enemy. Tenderly she prunes and prays. She knows that the ripening of this fruit is essential for your future prosperity and well-being. She is certain that you will need to feed on it and draw deeply on its strength if you are to fulfill all that God planned for your life. Each time you yield to God's mercy and love, she smiles her approval.

One day you discover that Brokenness has been planting a new kind of fruit in your heart. How often you have wanted to trust your Lord, taking your hands off His work, but you have not. Indeed, you are only too well aware of how many times you have tried to "help" God through some of the more difficult situations you and others have faced. Now, leaning heavily on the wisdom Brokenness has planted in your heart, you find yourself backing off and backing away. In fact, you are embarrassed to even think about forcing your will above God's will for your life and the lives of others. The mere thought of building your personal kingdom sends you to new depths of repentance and prayer, beseeching Him to prevent such a thing from happening again in your heart. Painfully you allow His purposes to supersede your own, and you put His Kingdom above your kingdom.

The mere thought of building your personal kingdom sends you to new depths of repentance and prayer.

Yes, something very real and very grand is happening in your heart. Without effort, you respond to others with greater compassion and more mercy. You find yourself understanding and being patient when others do not live up to your plan for their lives. You even find yourself relinquishing your plan for their lives and turning that very special, very eternal job over to the Lord.

"Thank you," the Lord says when you return His people to Him, allowing Him to be their Lord.

"I'm sorry about that," you mumble. "You see, I didn't understand that..."

"You've no need to explain," the Lord inter-
rupts. "Just don't try to take them back. You can't
have them."

Brokenness encourages you through these
difficult times of waiting and patience. When you
would yield to the temptation to judge another or
to be jealous of his good fortune, Brokenness leads
you to the place of intercession, far from the chambers of gossip and slander. With the memory of
your own struggles and your continual need of
mercy and forgiveness planted firmly in your
mind, she shows you the sin of your words,
thoughts, or attitudes until you are appalled at how
easily gossip, slander, and self-righteous anger rule
your life. Then you are not quite so quick to be
appalled when these faults show up in the lives of
other believers.

*Brokenness encourages you through
these difficult times of waiting
and patience.*

Daily, Brokenness faithfully holds a mirror
before you, lest you become too indignant at the
failures of others. Seeing your own face shuts you
up every time. "Yes, Lord!" you respond. "Thank

You for Your mercy!" Then, with the memory of your failures fresh in your mind, you go back to pray for the weakness you have detected in another. This time, however, your prayer is bathed in kindness and understanding because Brokenness has caused you to see and understand the work of the Cross in your own life.

Now the way you treat people changes dramatically. You are surprised to find that you respond with a compassion, mercy, and love that you never thought possible. Repentance fills your heart when you see how wrong you have been, and you remember the many times you have been far too quick to judge, far too quick to equate the sin with the person who is sinning, far too quick to banish, shun, and turn the sinner over to satan. You wonder when you decided that it was easier and less painful to disregard the one with sin instead of trying to redeem him.

The power of Brokenness is also evident in the new eyes with which you see the miracle of repentance. You are astonished at how wondrously the Lord uses repentance to isolate the corruption of sin, applying His own precious blood to wrap up your iniquity, covering it completely until He can thoroughly remove the damage sin has wrought. How carefully He keeps it under control until loving and nonjudgmental parts of His Body come gently beside you and remove it once and for all from your life.

Yes, true Brokenness is the mercy of God flowing from your heart to other folks who are struggling with sin. It's not that Brokenness seeks to hide the sin, but her nearness prompts you to embrace the one who is struggling, to say, "I know what you are going through; I'm sorry it hurts," and to truly mean it because you have been there, and maybe are still there. Oh, your sin may not have been made public, but you know that you too could very easily have been caught. You too could be in the place of the person who needs your mercy.

True Brokenness is the mercy of God flowing from your heart to others who are struggling with sin.

The compassion of Brokenness inspires you to offer mercy in the same way you need mercy. Your heart is softer when she is near. Like no other, she constrains you to encourage others in their battles against sin and to stand alongside them in their moments of failure. Your lips are opened to recount the reality of your own struggles, and your heart empathizes because you have had similar experiences. Even now you know that you struggle with problems that are every bit as serious as the failure facing the one to whom you are called to show mercy.

This is the power behind Jesus' mercy, the power released in true Brokenness. Jesus became human and experienced everything you face so that He could feel with you and for you. Brokenness gives you the same power to share the struggles of others. She teaches you that all men and women are fellow strugglers. Daily she reminds you that mercy cannot be released from a place of lofty pride. Always she is ready to free you from an attitude of superiority or self-promotion. As Brokenness reminds you who you are apart from Christ, you realize the futility of exalting yourself above another and of promoting yourself and your gifts. You understand that we all have a piece of the truth that we must fit into what others see.

We all have a piece of the truth that we must fit into what others see.

Now you have the courage and the compassion to reach out to God's people. For when she is near, Brokenness draws God's people together and to their knees, fervently praying for one another and for a lost world that desperately needs a people who have discovered her power.[1]

WHOLENESS AND BROKENNESS

Isn't it amazing that I start a chapter on wholeness by talking about brokenness? Yet, wholeness emerges from brokenness. Wholeness, when God is making you whole, is a completion of soul and spirit that can only be accomplished by the Cross. For many, brokenness is where the process ends. Its pain is too difficult and its process too unbearable.

I understand. Brokenness is a word that I have feared for many years. I did my best to avoid it. But, and I say this cautiously, I am glad brokenness caught up to me. In fact, it did not catch up with me, it ran me over as I went recklessly into the realms of spirit that I knew little about and was completely unprepared to understand and deal with. I had spent my life mimicking those I admired and found myself powerless and empty. I can say that I understand how the seven sons of Sceva felt when they confronted demons without brokenness:

> *Some wandering Jews were also trying to make evil spirits go out of people. The seven sons of Sceva were doing this. (Sceva was an important Jewish priest.) These Jews were using the name of the Lord Jesus to do this. They all said, "By the same Jesus whom Paul proclaims, I order you to come out!" One time, an evil spirit said to these Jews, "I have heard about Jesus, and I know Paul, but who are*

you?" Then the man who had the evil spirit jumped on these Jews. He was much stronger than they were. He beat them up and tore off their clothes. They ran away from that house (Acts 19:13-16).

No, avoiding the process of brokenness is not the recommended way of maturity. Through brokenness, we are retooled by the Spirit of the Lord so the Presence of Jesus can shine brightly with all His love, mercy, and compassion. The more we yield to Him, the more we shine with Him. The more we accept our weakness, the stronger we become in Him.

This is why, for Christ, I can take pleasure in weaknesses, insults, hardships, persecutions, and disasters. Because when I am weak, that's when I am really strong (2 Corinthians 12:10).

Hmmm, this reminds me of another important Scripture, "Humble people are happy, because the earth will be given to them" (Matt. 5:5).

Chapter 5

THE LOVE SHACK MEANS REFRESHING RESTORATION

The following story is taken from my book *Secrets of the Most Holy Place, Volume Two,* and depicts the way we need to be restored *beyond* restoration. Just as God restored to Job more than he had lost, God makes it His desire to bring more than we deserve into our reality.

> The same thing happened every school day morning. My twin brother, Ron, and I would grab our coats out of the closet off the old metal hangers and run down the driveway to catch our ride to school. The force of the coats being pulled off the hangers would send them flying in every direction as we slammed the closet door. We had a good laugh listening to those old hangers banging around the closet as we ran out of the house.

Our family wasn't poor, but that was only because our parents were very careful with everything we had. Our stuff always lasted much longer than it should have. In fact, if yard sales had been popular in those days, I am sure we never would have had one at our house. The things we had were used until they completely fell apart after being glued together several times. They would have been totally useless to anyone else. So when Ron and I came home one night and found our two old metal coat hangers bent like boomerangs and sitting on the kitchen table, we knew there was going to be a talk.

We couldn't help but laugh when we saw those hangers sitting there. They had finally had enough of our pulling at them, bending them, and sending them knocking around the closet every day. They were near the breaking point, pitiful looking.

Every time we pulled our coats off the hangers, we put stress at the same spot. Over time that one spot became too weak to do its job. The inevitable happened. The hangers became permanently bent. Eventually it didn't matter if we were careful to straighten the hangers before we put the coats on them, the weight of the coats was enough to bend them. For a long time, we could make the hangers straight so they looked like nothing was wrong. But then the metal began to turn white, a sign of the stress it was under each time we tugged a coat off. Even though we could get the hangers to straighten out, we would never get the color or the strength back into those two old hangers.

Now, I don't know how much hangers cost in those days, but it didn't much matter—we were going to hear about it. As was our custom when things looked bleak for us, we sat mischievously quiet, very close to angel-like as we heard Dad's old panel truck pulling into the driveway. I had no idea that he was about to teach me something that would turn out to be one of the most important lessons I would ever learn.

Dad walked up the stairs into the kitchen, where he knew we would be waiting.

"Hi, Dad, we had a great day at school today! Have any chores for us?"

"Right." We knew he was holding back a smile. He was that kind of dad.

"Boys, we are going to talk about these old hangers. You have to be careful how you treat them."

Here goes, I thought. One time, I kicked my brother under the table to get him to laugh, but he completely ignored me. So I kicked him again and again. I wanted him to be the first one to crack a smile. He was.

"Son," Dad turned toward me, "is there something wrong with your foot?"

"No, Dad."

"Then you better hold it still before you put a hole in my leg."

I froze, but he went on eating without another word.

"Boys, you just can't keep bending these hangers in the same spot like this. You are going to break it for sure. The metal just cannot handle that kind of treatment. Take care of it, be gentle, and it will stay strong forever."

"But, Dad, it's just a hanger." We tried not to laugh.

"It's not just a hanger. It has value and it can be fixed. If something can be fixed, boys, it's worth saving. Let me show you."

We followed Dad down to his workshop. He pulled two ten-penny nails out of an old coffee can and fired up his welder.

We watched as he carefully straightened out the hangers and then spot-welded the nails across the weakened part of both hangers. The weak area became the strongest part of the hanger. It was amazing, to be sure. I used that same hanger for years. It never bent there again. In fact, it was clearly the strongest part of the hanger.

"That old hanger won't be strong there again," he said to us. "But that ten-penny nail will be its strength. It'll surely break somewhere else before it breaks where I just fixed it. The weakest part is now the strongest part."

I don't know what Dad understood about iniquity, but I got the message years later as I lamented before the Lord over my own struggle.

Iniquity Enters

The more I sin in a particular fashion, the weaker I get at that spot in my life. Temptation in that area results in sin far more often as my ability to resist diminishes. I'm like that old hanger that kept being bent in the same way, time after time. I can be strong in so many other ways, but in the thing I give in to the most, my weakness grows. Temptation and sin are turned into iniquity there, a weakness toward a sin I cannot resist and certainly cannot overcome.

I need a ten-penny nail over that weak spot. I cannot protect myself there anymore. I have given in too many times. I need the power of the Cross, my eternal ten-penny nail, welded over my weakness so I can be strong again. With this power of Christ Himself, I can now resist the very thing that enslaved me.

In the Holy Place, we just rebuke the devil and make as many excuses as are necessary to satisfy the conscience. But my weakness is forever weak, forever a place where I am certain to fall, forever in a place where I come short of His glory.

My Ten-Penny Nail

But in the Most Holy Place, [our personal Love Shack], where the Mercy Seat calls to us and His power is made perfect in weakness, the work of Christ goes beyond our weak and fleshly attempts to make restitution and cover our own sins. This is where our confession, complete and without reservation, releases the power of God to become our ten-penny nail. Truly, where I was weak, I am now strong. Though I may occasionally fall, His mercy is ever present to wash me with His blood and gather me to Himself. Here, in His manifest Presence, I have no fear and therefore no need to make an excuse. His love overwhelms me and I am confident that I can confess my sin freely and without blame toward another. I am responsible for my sin.

But here there is no condemnation and no fear. He will not condemn what He has redeemed. He will not scatter what He has gathered. I have passed from death to life. My weakness becomes my strength. My failure becomes a testimony of my hope, for He will never leave me.

Rather, His power gathers where I fail. He holds my weakness in the palm of His hand, strengthening me in my hope of deliverance.

Now, sin is no longer master over me. I am no one's slave, no one's puppet. My life is now and forever hidden in the Christ of God, whose power and deliverance was purchased for me completely on the Cross. He is my hope and my strength. He is my ten-penny nail.[1]

"T'ROW THE BALL!"

Sometimes when we know something that others don't, we have a tendency to get puffed up. At times we lord our knowledge over others—perhaps on purpose, perhaps not. During God's restoration process we need to be open to His plan—wide open. The following true story from *Secrets of the Most Holy Place, Volume Two,* hits that principle home.

I knew he had something exciting to tell me. I could see it in his huge brown eyes as I pulled into the driveway that beautiful spring evening after work. As usual, his brothers raced to the car with tales of adventure and intrigue that filled their day, all talking and laughing at the same time. Soon, having stolen sufficient hugs and kisses for the time being, they ran off to discover who knows what in the wooded fields behind our home.

Then there was Joel. After patiently waiting for his brothers to leave, he walked toward me with anticipation and excitement in his eyes. He was only seven, but his eyes always told a dozen stories and revealed a hundred secrets. He threw his arms around me.

"Dad, guess what?"

"Hi, Joel, what do you want me to guess?"

"Guess what I want to do?"

"Hmmm, guess what you want to do…"

"I want to play baseball! I was talking to my friend, and he's playing and he wants me to play too."

"Baseball! That's great, son! That's awesome."

"But Dad, I don't know how to play baseball."

I couldn't help laughing. "That's OK, son. I

will teach you. Tomorrow is Saturday. We'll start tomorrow." He was so excited.

Early the next morning we rummaged through the garage until we found all the necessary equipment for a good series of lessons. Back outside, Joel grabbed the bat and held it over his shoulder. "I want to hit the ball," he said with devilish determination. I laughed.

He stood in front of me swinging the bat so hard he nearly knocked himself over. I started to review all the basics of the game. There was so much to talk about, so much he needed to know.

I talked on and on as I held the ball in my hand. Joel practiced the dozens of poses he had seen the pros do. He bent his knees and wiggled his little behind. He leaned over and stood up tall. He spit in his hands and rubbed them in the dirt, then wiped them on his legs. He was already playing baseball.

"Why do guys spit in their hands?" he interrupted me.

"It helps them grip the bat," I responded, watching him peel the mud from between his fingers. "But they don't usually spit that much in their hands."

"Kinda gross," he mumbled as he knelt down and tried to wipe his hands clean on the grass.

"Pay attention now, son."

"Sure, Dad," he said as he rubbed the bat under his arm like the big guys do.

I didn't stop to realize that he had no idea what I was saying. He was riveted with the anticipation of swinging that stick and hearing the crack of the bat as the ball soared over the house and beyond.

Nonetheless, there was so much he needed to know. I just kept talking, quite proud of everything I knew about the game and completely absorbed in my exhaustive presentation.

The sound of a small boy whimpering interrupted my discourse. I was aghast as I saw Joel standing in front of me crying. Only moments before, he was having so much fun thinking about swinging the bat. Now he was leaning on it as he cried.

"What's the problem, Joel? I thought you were excited about learning to play baseball. I thought you wanted me to teach you to..."

"Just t'row the ball, Dad! T'row the ball!"

I was shocked and embarrassed. I suddenly realized that the learning would come with the playing. In fact, learning seemed secondary to his desire to play. But playing would increase his desire to learn.

I dropped the ball and gathered him in my arms. As always during times of childhood trauma, he buried his face in my neck. I couldn't help but laugh at myself.

"Was Daddy talking too much?"

He never said a word, but I could feel his head nodding.

"I am so sorry, son. Come on, now, pick up that bat and let's see how far you can hit this ball."

In an instant, he jumped out of my arms, grabbed the bat, put it over his shoulder, and looked at me with that familiar devilish grin. He was about to hit that ball to kingdom come or fall down trying, but he was going to be playing baseball.

Waiting to Play Ball

Joel is not the only one who is waiting to play ball. I can remember sitting in more church meetings than I can count, just waiting for the preacher to "t'row the ball." In fact, like my son, I have been exasperated to tears as apparently crucial instruction was given in drone-like perfection week after week, month after month, and year—well, you get the picture.

The Church has been waiting for years for someone to just shut up and "t'row the ball." We have believed in authority and patiently waited for men and women of God to release us into all that God has dreamed for us. We have waited to be released by the power of the prophetic word that sets hearts ablaze with the possibility of doing the will of God and fulfilling our destiny at long last.

Nonetheless, believers are still waiting for someone to empower them. We are waiting for someone to remind us that God loves us and not only has a dream for us as individuals, but fully intends to see those dreams come to pass while we are able to do something about them. But, alas, the ball cannot be thrown by the worn and tired prayers of a clueless religious system, or the eloquent sermons that are presented with breathless precision. The ball cannot be thrown by people who build their kingdoms and are buried in their own insecurities. The ball will never be thrown by hirelings who are primarily concerned with their positions and their own futures.

Who Wants to Play Ball?

The ball can only be thrown by people who want you to play the game. It can only be thrown by those who are more interested in the Church than their own egos. The leaders who want you to participate have no agenda and no fear of being outplayed. They are not afraid of throwing the ball to a better player. They rejoice that Christ will be more magnificently displayed. These folks have only one goal. They are desperate for the reality and love of Christ Jesus Himself who is the Bread of Life to the nations and the Living Water who quenches the thirsty soul.

I can say this so confidently because Jesus already threw the ball when He gave Himself for us and rose so victoriously from the dead. You are the priest of the Presence. You are the royal priesthood, the holy nation. You are already the minister of His glory whether or not you are ever recognized or ordained by anyone. He has seen you, recognized you, and called you to Himself. You may never stand in a pulpit or teach a Sunday school class, but you minister His Presence because He lives in you. The dream God has dreamed for humankind can only be fulfilled when we all step forward and become everything that He has placed in our hearts to be as individuals.

The dream God has dreamed for humankind can only be fulfilled when we all step forward and become everything that He has placed in our hearts to be as individuals.

Some will be ready for this; others will be caught looking in another direction. But we will "t'row the ball." Many of us are waiting for the opportunity, the possibility of intimate fellowship, friendship, and service to our Lord that will last for the rest of our lives. We are the ones who understand that we are priests of the Presence, the Body of Christ, the Melchizedek of God. We are God's intended instruments of mercy, love, and salvation. We are the lamps in whom dwells the Light of the World.

The Beginning of Dreams
What God has done for us is not the sum of our

dreams—it is the beginning of them. It is not the final destination—it is where we discover the dream He has for us and then agree with that dream.

This Most Holy Place, [your personal Love Shack], is certainly where we rest in Him, but it is far from a resting place.

From this position of attentive eagerness, He speaks what you have longed to hear. It is in this place where you are quick to say yes to what He wants. He launches you with His faith, His power, and His confidence. You soon find your life full of meaning and purpose. But it is not the *place* that brings ultimate fulfillment. Ultimate fulfillment is found by doing the will of God once you have experienced this place of profound peace. This makes life worth living, no matter what it might be that He has dreamed for you.

No, I will not lie and tell you that not playing will cost your salvation, for then I would be no different from the religious taskmasters who force their desires on you through fear and intimidation. No, resisting Him will not cost your salvation, but it may cost your sense of fulfillment and joy as you see His Kingdom established *around* you instead of *through* you.

This is not a call to church. It is a call to His Presence and to the Church that He is building, wherever on this planet that may be. This is a different challenge. It is not a challenge simply to agree with the words that are written. It is a challenge to allow the heart fire that these words will undoubtedly ignite, to cause you to move beyond hearing and even beyond believing. These words should move you into doing, thus finding yourself in the very center of His work on this planet.[2]

He has every confidence in you.

RESTORATION

The dream of brokenness is one we have all dreamed. How we wake up from it makes all the difference. This excerpt from *The Power of Brokenness* illustrates how restoration and wholeness walk hand in hand.

"I have a dream," Brokenness whispers one morning when you join her at your usual meeting place. The mist of the breaking dawn is still pouring off the mountains as the first rays of the sun warm your chilled faces. "It is a grand dream. Would you like to hear it?"

"Oh yes," you eagerly agree.

"I dream of a day when the people of God have completely given themselves to the power of Brokenness. There will be not only one person here and one person there, but a visible company of believers devoted only to our Lord. There will be no imposters, no one wearing masks, no one forcing his own way.

"I dream of a highway there, a highway of

holiness where the unclean cannot walk and no lion can prey on His godly ones. I dream of a people who yearn for God's love and who live under the influence of His compassion. This people heals, mends, forgives, and speaks Good News to the poor. They lean heavily on Brokenness, for they are constantly reminded of their need apart from their Lord. They do not forget who they are once they have seen themselves in the mirror Brokenness holds before them.

"Come to the place I have prepared for you, a mansion not in Heaven, but in the Spirit."

"I dream of a people who will leap at the sound of His voice, 'Come up hither. Come to the place I have prepared for you, a mansion not in Heaven, but in the Spirit. Come sit at My right hand so that I can teach you of My ways, that you may walk in My path, for from here I will send you to the four corners of the earth, as sowers go out to sow. You will water your seed with the tears of your intercessory prayer as I water the ground with the Holy Spirit. With great joy you will see fruit miraculously arise from the ground.'

"I dream of a people of God who rejoice with great delight as they see His Kingdom grow, even when that growth is through another. They encourage one another, pray for one another, and genuinely share in one another's victories. I dream of a people who know that their times are in the hands of their Lord. They rest with confidence and full assurance knowing that He has laid a plan that they cannot improve upon and that He is directing their future. So they rest in Him, waiting for the sound of His voice and doing with all their heart, without bitterness or regret, whatever is before them to do.

"I dream of a day when the graveyards of this world will no longer hold prisoner the creativity, passion, and tenacity that God gave to humanity to bless the world. No plan God has designed will go uncompleted, no hope will remain unfulfilled, no dream will end before it is finished because this fellowship of saints, composed of ordinary men and women throughout the earth who have abandoned themselves completely to God's plan, will arise with a passion and a commitment to do whatever God requires of them. Their ability, magnified by their union with God through His indwelling Spirit, will surpass anything this world has ever seen, or could ever hope to see.

"I dream of a day when true Brokenness releases the blessings God has planned to be poured on His people in a deluge of supernatural power and glory. In this day, there will be people who are not immobilized by the reality of their humanity. They will have learned that yielding to God, not perfection, is the requirement for destiny. For these folks, holiness becomes the lifestyle of desire, instead of a yoke of legalism."

Brokenness stands now and turns to face you. "I dream of the appearance of these people of God. They will come in all colors, sizes, and shapes, and they will not judge by what they see on the outside. Some will be very young, and others will be very old. They will walk in true unity and love, for the Lord Himself will have melded their hearts together through the power of Brokenness."

Brokenness looks off into the morning sky. "I can see them. They are not far off. These people understand that they will experience this *now*, in this life. His anointing will flow through them freely—convicting, healing, comforting, reconciling—for they will have long ago given up the right of their own will to embrace His. No personal plans, no individual preferences will restrict the free flow of the Holy Spirit, for these people will be completely sold out to God, delighting to obey His every bidding.

"And you, my child," Brokenness whispers again, enfolding you tenderly into her arms, "can be part of this majestic company who will soon subdue the earth with His glory, preferring Him above all others, placing His will above your own, and honoring His dreams even when they may dash yours.

"Self-promotion, personal agendas, and hidden motives have no place here. These vestiges of self-will shut out the very God who calls you. They exclude you from advancing His Kingdom.

"This, my child," Brokenness concludes, "is the Kingdom of which I dream. His Kingdom is advancing, visible in the hearts and lives of men and women like you who have chosen to embrace Brokenness and to respond to the gentle nudges of the Holy Spirit deep in their hearts. For wherever soft hearts give the Spirit of God room to live and work, wholeness and joy are the inevitable results.

"Thus God's people, those who have made a covenant with Him by sacrifice, cannot help but experience whatever God is doing, longs to do, and most certainly will continue to do. This, my friend, is truly the power of Brokenness."[3]

Complete restoration of our relationship with our heavenly Father is found in the Love Shack. It is not hidden in the closet or under the rug. Restoration is found in every nook and cranny of the place He calls you to be—where He wants you to live with Him. No searching required. Acceptance of His love and mercy will soften your heart enough to absorb His Presence.

WHAT ABOUT TODAY?

In *Secrets of the Most Holy Place*, I discuss the wonders of Christ within and reveal how we don't have to put our desires on hold—they can and should be realized now, today.

Am I really experiencing this? you ask yourself one day. *Is this depth of relationship really possible?* You have often heard of those who talked about the deeper Christian life, and you wondered if it were truly possible to experience such a life on this side of eternity. But here you are, enjoying an intimacy and depth of fellowship with the Lord that you had only dreamed of. [You are enjoying life with your Lord in your personal Love Shack.]

You have taken that step of abandonment. You have given all. You have stepped into Him—and it is wonderful. You can feel yourself changing as you see Him moment by moment. You never dreamed that there were so many wonderful things He wanted you to know. You recall with amazement a promise He made to you not very long ago. "The secret of the Lord is for those who fear Him, and He will make them know His covenant." And what a covenant! How powerful! How far beyond anything our human minds can conceive or understand!

Now you are consumed with the burning, almost painful desire to love Him even more completely. "More than anything, I want to know You. More important than anything material is the desire to know You, my Lord. You." Your most sincere prayers bring quick response from a Lord who delights in showing Himself to His people.

But are you sure you are ready for Him to pull back the curtain of eternity just a little, so that you may truly see things as they really are? For things as they are in God are not always as they are perceived by us. Nonetheless, there is nothing that compels you more than your desire to know Him and to see Him.

But are you sure you are ready for Him to pull back the curtain of eternity just a little, so that you may truly see things as they really are?

The one question that you were always positive you would ask the Lord, given the opportunity and right circumstances of course, now seems so unnecessary, so out of place. It is not at all that you no longer care when His Second Coming will be; it is simply that there is now more than His Second Coming to consider. Yes, there will be a literal Second Advent; but you are beginning to understand that the burden of responsibility is not on Him as much as it rests upon each generation.

Each generation is responsible for His appearing in that time. He has a master plan. Each generation holds an awesome responsibility in that plan. Each must fulfill what they were born to accomplish. Each generation must do what God has determined in His heart for them to do. How clearly you see it now. Oh, how simple to merely look for a physical

Second Coming far off in the future! But what a burden that puts on posterity. We have pointed to tomorrow, to some future generation, and demanded from them a level of faith and revelation we have not been willing to find for ourselves.

What about today? you ask yourself.

"Well, what *about* today?" you hear the Lord return the question. "Are you willing," He continues, "to consider for today all that you and your fathers have relegated to the future?" Suddenly, it dawns on you that Jesus preached that the Kingdom of God was at hand. John the Baptist preached the same message before Him. "I AM that I AM" the voice of the Lord thunders in your heart. "I am not the God of the dead, but of the living. *Today* if you hear My voice, do not harden your heart!"

We are beginning to see just how terribly irresponsible the Church has been throughout the centuries. How many promises have we neglected? How much of the New Covenant has been carelessly pushed into some elusive time period called the Millennium just because it was neither experienced nor understood by the Church at large? How much of God's intention for our generation do we quickly dismiss because a man said it was for another place and another time?

The challenge becomes too great. You cannot contain the shock of what you have just seen. "Lord! Lord!" you cry out. "Do not let me breathe my last breath until I have accomplished all that is on Your heart for me! I love Your appearing! But I love Your appearing most fully when You appear in the Church and Your people."

As we look back over the centuries, it becomes clear that God had a destiny for each generation. The purposes of some ages were more visible than others; some were more obedient than others. But at each revelation, at each appearing, carnal humankind took His precious secrets and hoarded them as though they were their own. As we were greedy for gain, His Covenant became a commodity to be merchandized to the world. Instead of becoming the Body of Jesus, sharing, growing, helping one another and encouraging one another, some began to buy and sell their little tidbits of truth as though they held the final word on His character and Person.

Instead of each generation gathering together to fast and pray, humbly seeking the Father, we have often retreated behind walls of doctrine and self-righteousness.

Instead of each generation gathering together to fast and pray, humbly seeking the Father, some have retreated behind walls of doctrine and self-righteousness, each raising high their own banner of truth and excellence. Outwardly portraying unity and brotherhood, all the while their hearts have lusted after the loftiest positions. Instead of possessing a standard of righteousness that could have established and reinforced His Kingdom in each generation, too many have gathered their dollars and built their own little kingdoms.

At a glance all these little worlds sound like Him. Some even look like Him. There are one or two that try to act like Him. But on much closer examination, they are seen to be whitewashed tombs devoid of life and possessing only the hollow sounds of a barren relationship and a bankrupt kingdom.

Chills run up your spine, and you shudder at these thoughts. But your spirit bears witness with God's Spirit. Your spirit burns with His as He shares with you these awesome secrets. Now you know. Now you are responsible. Now there can be no excuses. Now there can be no turning back. Each generation is responsible for His appearing in their generation. Each generation. Each generation. As it sinks into your spirit, you find yourself confessing, "My generation, my generation, my generation."

Oh, the purpose! Oh, the destiny! Oh, the burden He has given us! No wonder He says to us, "Go into your closet and shut the door!" No wonder He continually calls us to Himself! There is a destiny on our generation. There is something wrapped up in the heart of God Almighty that He has set aside for our generation to accomplish.

You are not renouncing past generations or their truths. To be sure, your destiny is wrapped in building upon what they have already done. Your destiny will add to their work as the next generations' will add to yours. But be sure to understand this. If you do not handle His appearing to your generation, but choose merely to live on what has been, it will taste worse than yesterday's manna.

Each generation is responsible for His appearing in their generation.

Do not be intimidated by those who will try to convince you that you have nothing to add. These are carnal people who oppose the genuine life of God, the growth that is yours because of Jesus Christ. These people write big, important-looking books, and bind them with expensive bindings. Even the appearance of these books can be intimidating, as they are intended to be. By the size of their books these people are telling you that what they have is final. But you know better. You know that truth is progressive. You know that every time you see Jesus you are changed a little more into His likeness and image.

Do not respond to these people, but respond to Him who is waiting to appear to your generation. He is waiting to appear to you. He is waiting to show you His Covenant. So respond to Him. Give in to His tugging on your heart.[4]

Find your prayer closet in the Love Shack, and shut the door behind you.

HEARTS ABLAZE

So now your spirit burns to know the ways of God. Your desire drives you to know His very secrets. I was right, was I not? I know you. I know your heart yearns for Him. I know, because my spirit burns like that too.

The ultimate pleasure in life is to know God's plan, to hear His voice, and to walk into all that He has destined for us to become. All other goals fade in the blaze of this desire. All other aspirations are insignificant by comparison.

The Always-Present One [tells] *His secrets to those who revere Him. He reveals His covenant to them* (Psalm 25:14).

You and I need to make a commitment. We need to have a mutual resolve in light of our new discoveries while journeying to the Love Shack. Are you ready?

You and I are finished comparing ourselves with other Christians. You and I are finished measuring our faith, our doctrines, and our dreams by others' standards. That feels right, doesn't it?

We now have dwindling interests in our needs, our reputation, and our pride. We are through trying to fulfill fleshly expectations and treading lightly upon the binding traditions of man. Remember, our hearts yearn for God, for the living God, and we resolve to find Him in an abandoned search for His fullness.

We have barely begun to understand the full provision of the New Covenant, let alone walk in it. We have barely begun to taste the goodness of the Lord that is ours through salvation in Jesus Christ. We have only tasted the fruit of genuine inheritance; we have barely understood the passion that our heavenly Father has in reaching out to us, or His love so intense, that He gave His only Son.[5]

There, we did it. Exhilarating, isn't it? We have made some decisions that will change us forever...just as He has always desired.

On our journey to the Love Shack we've discovered some simple secrets of the New Covenant that are ours within the veil, where He rules as Lord and King in His manifest Presence. If you are willing to step beyond the walls of traditionalism, even Charismatic traditionalism, you will find yourself stepping into a deeper realm of His Presence and a more excellent fellowship with God.

His Spirit within compels us to come deeper, to move past the familiar into a reality of supernatural love and power that is beyond our imagination. He is about to visit the earth once again, and He will do it as He is pleased to reveal Himself in you and me. He is about to unveil the fullness of His salvation to those who genuinely fear Him and long for His appearing.

I know you are one of those people.

Your heart gives you away.

Chapter 6

THE LOVE SHACK MEANS MERCY, COMPASSION, AND GRACE

Few understand the power of our judgments—or the aftermath of the words we speak in thoughtless, emotional pain. In my book *The Angel and the Judgment*, "The Preacher" comes face to face with his utterances and finally realizes the effect they have on the world.

THE PREACHER

"Room service! Oh, excuse me, sir, but did you order room service?"

Was he dreaming? Was he dead? Was he hallucinating?

"Oh, never mind, it must be the next body down the road a little," the angel said as he walked away.

The preacher could only groan. He forced his now cold, misshapen hand out just in time to brush the angel's leg.

The angel stopped abruptly and turned to the man of faith and power. He stood there a moment, wondering why a man would not allow his heart to melt before God. He knew he could never understand the awesome mysteries of salvation, but it still saddened him that humanity was so stubborn and arrogant.

It is a fearful thing to fall into the hands of an angry God, the angel thought. *I don't know everything, but I do know that it doesn't have to be this way.*

The angel finally broke the silence. "Well, so you are alive. I wonder how that happened? Everyone within a 60-mile radius of the explosion was slated to die. The Judgment, you know. The rain does certainly fall upon the just and the unjust, does it not? But we do have our quotas before it can officially be called the Judgment." The angel scanned the landscape, reviewing the countless bodies thrown like rag dolls over the land.

"Yes. Well, it's these humans, you know. They keep mixing up their own natural feelings with the compassion of God. Something doesn't go their way, and all they want is vengeance. 'Call down fire from Heaven,' they say. 'Send the Judgment,' they say. If they only knew what their lack of God's wisdom and rampant human fleshly emotions can cause."

The angel stopped only momentarily, nudging the preacher ever so slightly with his foot.

The preacher jerked like a man hit by a lightning bolt and then groaned with pain.

"Yes, well," the angel continued, "are you going to stay alive long enough for the next event? It gets much more exciting from here."

The preacher tried to speak, but his parched throat prevented him.

"What did you say?" The angel bent down to hear him. "Oh, I'm sorry, you must be desperately thirsty." The angel lifted a long-stemmed glass of ice water from a tray. The soothing moisture relieved the man's thirst and restored his damaged voice box enough to talk.

"The next event? You mean there is more? When is this all going to end?" he whispered as best he could.

"Well, sir, you have no idea how deep the mercy of God is. If His mercy prevails, I am sure it will last as long as it has to. God's mercy always has your best interest at heart," the angel replied.

"What are you talking about?" The preacher tried to sound confused, but it was a meager attempt, for they both knew better. The angel did not respond. It was certain that the only way this man would truly understand mercy would be to experience it himself. But he was not through with suffering quite yet.

"Please tell me I'm dreaming," the preacher whispered. "Please tell me I am still in the hotel room and that this is just a very bad dream."

The angel had an uncanny ability to ignore any question he deemed too ridiculous to answer. This was one of those moments when the whining would not be acknowledged.

"Does it hurt?" the angel asked with no pity and only a little sarcasm. "I thought you wanted the Judgment. I thought you were praying for it. Your mouth watered and your heart raced every time you talked about it. You had a gleam of utter satisfaction every time you walked off the platform, leaving the people with no hope and no answers. You loved painting a picture of God that was vengeful and morbid. You delighted in describing a god whose grace was limited and whose mercy was reserved for a select few who were just like you. Well, it seems to me that you got what you wanted."

The preacher rolled his eyes in pain. "Please. Please tell me this isn't happening."

"OK," the angel responded rather offhandedly. "It isn't happening."

"Thank God!" was all the preacher could say as he lay back on the ground, positioning himself to be, well, I guess he thought he would be transported back to his hotel.

The angel stood silently for a few minutes as the preacher continued to lie in pain. Finally he looked up in exasperated impatience.

"Are you there, angel?" he shouted.

"I am standing right here," the angel dutifully responded with an honorable salute.

"Why am I still here? Why am I still lying here in such terrible pain?"

"Well, I suspect it is because less than 60 miles away, one of your nasty human weapons of destruction exploded just a few hours ago, and you happened to be in the neighborhood. Excellent timing, if I do say so myself."

"But you said that it really didn't happen," the preacher protested.

"But that was only because you told me to tell you that."

The preacher lay in utter disbelief. "You can't be serious! This can't be real! You must make it go away! Take me back to the hotel!" His voice was all but gone again as he sobbed. He tried to wipe his eyes with his hands, only to feel the gritty asphalt melted into them.

"Oh, so now you want it to be a dream? Now you are concerned?" the angel queried. "You were the one preaching the Judgment. You were the one who begged God for this to happen," the angel tormented him.

"I never thought it would come to me! I never thought I would be judged. Surely God will have mercy. Surely there is room in His heart for forgiveness," the preacher said desperately to the angel.

"Mercy. Forgiveness. Strange coming from a man like you. Strange indeed. It has been a long time since words of that caliber passed through your lips. Mercy? Forgiveness? Don't you remember? Your god removed these words from his active file. They have no meaning now, do they?"

"I just do not understand," the preacher whined. "I just don't see why this is happening to me, of all people! Have mercy on me, O God!"

"You have denied God's mercy to a nation, and now you would ask for it yourself as if you have some special exemption?" the angel said. "Next you will be asking for His grace."

"Yes, oh yes, His grace would be so grand in an hour of torment such as this," the preacher said.

"And precisely where were your prayers for mercy and forgiveness when the Judgment fell on the others?" the angel asked.

"Well, they deserved it."

"And you don't?"

The preacher was silent, stunned by a view of himself he had, up until now, not taken the time to notice. There, in the silent torment of his own judgment, a miracle began to happen. In a very remote part of his heart, far from his own consciousness but close to the Spirit of the Lord, an ever-so-small miracle rooted. His heart began to soften.[1]

MERCY, COMPASSION, GRACE FOR ALL

If there is one thing for certain in the Love Shack, it is that our minds and hearts will certainly change. Experiencing His unending mercy and grace, we will see the world from His perspective. We will find ourselves loving, smiling, helping, and giving like never before. No longer will we be tossed from one emotion to another at the whim of mere mortals. No longer will our precious emotions, given by God to understand the depth of His personality and love for humanity, be used to force fleshly giving or sweaty servitude to a system or someone's personal kingdom. (Isn't it amazing that emotions are not allowed to be part of our Christian life unless we are being told a very touching—and probably untrue—story just to extort money, time, work, and talent from God's people?)

> *You, O One Who Is Always Present, give true (perfect) peace to those who depend on You, to those who trust in You. So, always trust the Always-Present One. Trust in Him because He is the Rock Eternal* (Isaiah 26:3-4).

You are just beginning to understand that all He has given to you is within your grasp. If only you would have had the eyes of your heart opened long ago to see the wonder, the security, the strength of His words, for they are not the random ramblings of an ancient, dusty book. They are the living Words of the living God in the here and now, in this dimension and every dimension of spirit and beyond. He cannot be moved... and neither can you.

Think about things that are above, not things on the earth. Since you have died, your life has been hidden away with Christ in God (Colossians 3:2-3).

The Holy Spirit tells us the truth. He tells us: "The Lord God says, 'This is the agreement I will make with them in the future: I will put My laws on their hearts. I will write My laws on their minds. I will forget about their sins and their wrongs'" (Hebrews 10:15-17).

Now your soul is resting in Him.

Now you see differently.

Now you see from His perspective.

And absolutely everything is different.

Open your heart. Open your mind. Open the eyes of your heart.

He is resting in your heart, the Most Holy Place, the Love Shack.

Don't act like people of this world. Instead, be changed inside by letting your mind be made new again. Then you can determine what is good, pleasing, and perfect—what God wants (Romans 12:2).

"Who can completely understand the Lord's mind? Who can give Him advice?" But we have the mind of Christ! (1 Corinthians 2:16).

Genuine mercy, compassion, and grace will send you to the

hungry, the poor, the sick, and the lonely. As you learn of Him, allowing Him total reign in your life, He will take you places that few would go unless He opened the doors.

Come with me as I continue the story of my venture behind the veil as told in *Romancing the Divine*.

ONE WITH GOD

He said, "You will learn and carry as your burden true love for all humanity, for we are becoming one. My ways are becoming your ways. Now the love you have is the same love that I have for the world.

"It is a love that blesses and does not curse.

"It is a love that gathers and does not scatter.

"It is a love that forgives and never holds retribution in its heart.

"It is a love that covers and heals.

"It is a love that cannot be imitated.

"It is a love that cannot be taken away, for it endures forever and grows stronger and stronger with each passing day until at last you cry out with joy and liberty, 'It is no longer I who live, but it is Christ who lives in me, and the life I am leading, I am leading by the faith of the Son of God who loved me and gave Himself for me.'"

What God showed and told me was so incredible. My heart raced with anticipation of all He had said to me. This is what I had yearned for and desired for so long. Now, it seemed as though it was all within the possibilities of His love. I wanted to ask more questions, but the Lord did not allow me to even try.

"No more questions now. Be at rest, My son, and be encouraged. The greatest adventure of your life is just beginning. You have only entered the doorway."

Well, I knew that was true. Just one look around the Most Holy Place proved that. This is undoubtedly the most amazing thing I have ever seen.

The Lord turned to me. "You are impressed with this? Wait until you see all this descending into the hearts of men and women around the world. That is a sight to behold.

"You will soon discover the life and the splendor that union produces. Son, you are done working for yourself. Now you really do belong to Me, not just by doctrine, but in reality. And what you have always hoped for will come to pass. We have much to do together."

I did not want to do anything or to go anywhere or to see anything else right now. I was quite content to stay just where I was. I had no interest in further adventures. I was happy to be in His Presence, safe and secure.

"You will not leave this place ever again. But there is much more, My son."

The Lord spoke with such thrilling encouragement. But I was tired of working. If I did anything else or went anywhere else, He would have to not only lead me, He would have to go with me.

"I will do more than go with you, My son. You will never work apart from Me. We will work in harmony in all we accomplish. Everything you do, you will do in Me. Everything I will do, I will do through you."

"Sounds like synchronized swimming to me."

"No, this is not synchronized swimming," the Lord laughed out loud, shaking His head. "You are just beginning to discover the essence of union and the reality of true destiny."

I stared at Him for a moment in sheer wonder that God might enjoy being with me as much as I enjoyed being with Him. More than that, He wanted to actually live and love and heal the nations *through* me. Incredible!

The Lord watched me and waited for me to recover from that most wonderful revelation. "Religion is satisfied for you to look like Me and act like Me. The outer appearance is everything to that system. But from the beginning, it was not to be this way. From the beginning, there would be a people who would yield to Me, trust Me, love Me. There would be a people through whom I would show Myself to the world, pouring out My love, My compassion, and My desire."

"Yes, Lord, this is what I want, what I live for. I want to please You, to give myself to You."

"And so you shall, so you shall."[2]

TANGIBLE RESULTS

The Love Shack gives us, for the first time, the hope, the opportunity to see tangible results of our walk with the Lord. While it is true that we walk by faith, at some point the faith by which we walk should demonstrate the results of that faith in ways that prove the power and love of the Lord in our lives. As the Lord lives His life through us, the power of eternity flows through us and we begin to see God's power toward all we touch.

We should not make excuses as to why we do not see the results of our faith. When what we believe doesn't deliver noticeable results, we must be mature and humble enough to re-examine what we have believed. The failure to do that is why there are so many powerless doctrines and belief systems in Christianity.

But suffice it to say that God's life moves through brokenness and His power is seen in lives open to His unpredictable ways.

Unless I am mistaken, you are one of those people who yearn to confound the wise and restore the broken and needy.

You will love the Love Shack!

Chapter 7

NEXT STOP—
THE LOVE SHACK

"OK," you are no doubt asking at this point, "Where is the Love Shack? How do I get there, and how do I establish my permanent residence there?"

The answers will both surprise and excite you, I am certain. It is nearer than you think and more tangible than you can accept.

First, let me tell you *what* the Love Shack is and then we will talk about *where* it is.

The Love Shack *is* the Most Holy Place. The original Most Holy Place was within the ancient Hebrew temple, the Tabernacle of Moses. It is important to have a very simple understanding of this shadow God used. This tabernacle is a type of the human body under the Old Covenant and is used in the Old Testament to describe our relationship to God and how we as individuals fit into His plan for humanity.

So look at this wonderful picture God has painted for us.

The Tabernacle of Moses consisted of three main divisions: the outer court, the inner court (the Holy Place), and the Holy of

Holies (the Most Holy Place). We (humans) are also three parts: body, soul, and spirit. These three rooms in the tabernacle each had unique characteristics and purposes in ancient times; even today they still have important significance and relevance as they depict different levels and aspects of our relationship with God. The three distinct parts of humankind also have unique characteristics and purposes and help us understand how we relate to God.

THE OUTER COURT

The outer court of the tabernacle was the place where sacrifices were made in an effort to find God's forgiveness. It represents man's attempts to reach God on his own. Without the aid of a Redeemer, man tries everything he can to please God. His life, therefore, is spent in uncertainty and unfulfillment.

Remember that we are also comprised of three parts: body, soul, and spirit. Our body is like the outer court of the tabernacle. It is farthest away from God and is interested only in its own self-preservation. The body acts in its own best interest and has no contact with God, just as those in the outer court of the tabernacle had no divine contact.

Outer court lifestyle is the "kingdom of self," not the Kingdom of God, and all its desires are self-centered and focused on the fulfillment of selfish desires. It is a fleshly realm, a place where people are in charge of their own lives. Instead of enjoying the benefits of the Kingdom of God, people in the outer court are focused on the struggles and conflicts that are part and parcel of self-centered living. They consider themselves on their own in their search for meaning and destiny.

THE HOLY PLACE

The next division of the tabernacle is the inner court, or the Holy Place. The Holy Place in the Tabernacle of Moses is where man meets the symbols that represent God's nature and His plan, but never really touches Him.

The Holy Place is a type of our intellectual assent. We see, we believe in our minds, accepting the logic of salvation and the tremendous good the principles of the Bible can do, but there is no true interaction with the living God; rather, in the middle room of the tabernacle, we interact with things of God rather than God Himself.

For soulish people, emotion trumps reality, doctrine trumps relationship, and religious precepts determine the activity of God. All these limit the eternal nature of the Lord and withhold the vast majority of all that God wants to do in our lives.

There is no way we can adequately comprehend the incredible richness of the salvation bought for us by Jesus on the Cross. When we are limited to the five senses and the limitations of the mind, we miss almost everything. Remember that between the Holy Place and Most Holy Place there was an 11-layer-thick curtain. There were no seams in it, and it ran from ceiling to floor. There was no way in or out of the Most Holy Place...until Jesus came and ripped the curtain from top to bottom, opening the way for all humankind to experience the fullness of our Lord in His marvelous glory.

There are no words that can describe the measure of our salvation. There are no adjectives to describe the depths of His love or the determination of His heart to bring us into the literal completion of His plan *in this life*. Check out these Scriptures:

Glory to God! He is able to do so much more than we can even think of or ask for. God uses the power that is working in us. Glory to God among all the people He has called out and in Christ Jesus for all generations forever and ever. Amen (Ephesians 3:20-21).

This gracious love was given to me, even though I am the least important of all the holy people. God wanted to preach the unsearchable riches of Christ to non-Jewish people. He wanted to teach everyone about the meaning of the secret plan. It was hidden in God a long, long time ago. (He created everything.) Why was it hidden? So that, through the people whom God called out, His many kinds of wisdom could be made clear to rulers and powers in the heavenly world (Ephesians 3:8-10).

HOW ARE WE TO THINK?

In this dimension, this "middle earth," humankind is aware of God and our conscience draws us toward the Lord, but our self-centeredness draws us away. It is here in the mind that the battle rages: self against God, good against evil, right against wrong, personal kingdom against the Kingdom of God. In this place between self-centered thinking and Christ-centered reality, we cannot decide who we want to follow.

There are days when our spirits are strong and we can withstand the temptations of the evil one. Other days our weaknesses seem to surface for no apparent reason. During these weak times, evil gets the upper hand and rules our hearts. This conflict is constant because in this realm we never make a final decision to follow the Lord at all costs. We never really yield our lives, futures, and desires to God. Deep inside, we still feel as if we know best what we need and how best to get it. We lack trust in the Lord. We are not certain that God knows best, nor are we certain that we really want what God wants for us. So we pray carefully. We ask for the things we want and avoid the things we know we really need and what is best for us in our hearts. So the battle rages in our minds until we reach a place of total surrender to Him.

We ask for the things we want and avoid the things we know we really need and what is best for us in our hearts.

In this division of the tabernacle, we are not really sure who we are or what we want to be. Somehow, we know we are supposed to be involved with the building of God's Kingdom, but we want to build our own kingdom at the same time. We want to leave our own mark in the world. In the Holy Place we hear God tell us to do something, but we still want to do what we want to do. Therefore, it is a place of great conflict, struggle, and mixture. We will never go where we know we want to be as long as indecision triumphs in us.

It is important to understand that I am not talking about going to Heaven when I discuss these things. The Scriptures are clear, "…'Commit yourself to the Lord Jesus and you will be saved—you and all the people living in your house'" (Acts 16:31). Rather, I am talking about experiencing the fullness of salvation in this life. Remember, Jesus taught us to pray, "May Your kingdom come. May what You want done be done. May it always be here on earth as it is in heaven" (Matt. 6:10).

The real estate of this Kingdom is in the heart of those who are open and willing.

Amazing. So many are waiting to go to Heaven while He is waiting for us to allow the Kingdom of God to come to us on earth. This mighty Kingdom does not have borders as nations of this world have borders. It does not have a prime minister, a president, or a king, as we define politics here on earth. The real estate of this Kingdom is in the heart of those who are open and willing. The king is King Jesus, and His throne is literally our hearts, the Most Holy Place, the Love Shack.

THE MOST HOLY PLACE

The third room of the Tabernacle of Moses was the Most Holy Place (the Holy of Holies). This is where God showed Himself to the High Priest once a year. It was a wonderful place of mercy, grace, blessing, and love. But for the Old Testament priests, it was a frightening and foreboding place. The priests did not understand the forgiveness of God or the power of the blood that was represented when they ventured beyond the veil.

This curtain, all 11 layers of it, represents our flesh and all the things in our hearts and minds that block our experience with God. When the curtain was torn in two, His Presence transcended dimensional limitations and opened our bodies, souls, and spirits to the fullest experience of God's love and purposes. He tore through our tunnel vision, our smallness. He opened a way to see Him as He truly is.

Christ is now the Risen King. His blood splashed through the Most Holy Place cleansing all people for all time and opening the entrance into the manifest Presence of the Lord where we are intended to enjoy unlimited fellowship and fulfillment. The way is prepared. We merely have to step beyond the veil of our fleshly limitations by faith in the atoning power of Jesus Christ.

That step of faith is a step of surrender to the will of God, trusting Him for everything.

That step of faith is a step of surrender to the will of God, trusting Him for everything. The power of the Most Holy Place (the Presence of God) is love, for God is love (see 1 John 4:8), and if you are in His Presence, you are enveloped by His love, and your heart responds to His love with love. It is there where you know that the most excellent way of all (see 1 Cor. 12:31) is to love God with all your heart, soul, and spirit and to love your neighbor as yourself (see Matt. 22:37-39).

In this dimension of "all God," your decision to follow Him is unchangeable. Sure you may falter, but your decision to follow Him and to trust Him with your future, as well as your present, never changes. This steadiness and determination brings a peace of mind and of heart that is beyond description. Now you don't spend time trying to get in relationship with God or fight to stay in relationship with Him. Now you can give yourself and your attention to His plan and work with Him to bring it to pass. You will no longer wonder if He will speak to you. You are simply quiet within your inner being so you can hear Him when He speaks.

The Most Holy Place is the place of fulfillment and certainty. This Most Holy Place, the Love Shack, is where destiny begins and grows into the fullest measure of its possibilities. The *ifs* disappear and are quickly replaced with *when*, and *when* gives birth to *hope* that causes a wellspring of worship and gratitude to pour from your heart.

You will no longer wonder if He will speak to you. You are simply quiet within your inner being so you can hear Him when He speaks.

Love in the Love Shack is the atmosphere in which you live and move and have your being. (See Acts 17:28.)

The Love Shack is a place of relationship where the believer draws close to God and God draws close to you. Oswald Chambers, in *My Utmost for His Highest*, writes:

> The most important aspect of Christianity is not the work we do, but the relationship we maintain and the surrounding influence and qualities produced by that relationship. That is all God asks us to give our attention to, and it is the one thing that is continually under attack.[1]

Maintaining our vital relationship with God involves entering His Presence and staying there. This is the wonderful benefit of being in the "yes" of God.

Many Christians talk about the power to heal, to cast out devils, and to raise the dead, but not as many talk about the power to love. If you pray for somebody in an effort to demonstrate the power to heal, you will miss the point. It is God's great love for the person that compels Him to move through you to bring healing to another. Jesus was moved with compassion. It was always out of His loving compassion that He ministered healing and hope to the people.

You can search for and have all the gifts of God and the gifts of the Holy Spirit and still fall short of His glory. The issue in God's heart is not how well you can impart His gifts, but how completely you let Him love the world through you.

When we let God love the world through us, many amazing things take place. As co-laborers with Him, we learn that He heals because He loves. He blesses because He loves. When we allow Him to move through us, we will love the world as He does, and we will freely scatter the seed of the Gospel everywhere, without thought of personal benefit. In fact, the purest ministry, the purest giving, is giving when the one receiving has no way to return the favor. This selflessness was first demonstrated by Jesus when He died for us on the Cross. It was an act born from a deep, abiding, and pure eternal love. There is nothing we can do to repay Him. He said, "You will be happier when you give than when you receive" (Acts 20:35).

The compassionate love of God drives us to reckless abandonment in our pursuit of Him as we carry the seed of His love to the four corners of the world.

In the Love Shack you can trust the Lord to take the seed wherever He wants it to go, and understand that the more seed you scatter, the more seed you will have. This is a law of the Kingdom of God. In fact, you will never run out of seed. The compassionate love of God drives you to reckless abandonment in your pursuit of Him as you carry the seed of His love to the four corners of the world.

There is a penetration of the Spirit of God that needs to occur within us, for this is what leads us to agree with God. The walls of resistance that we have built around our lives through the years need to come down. That will happen only in the Most Holy Place—in the manifest Presence of God—in the Love Shack. Here, we are humbled. Here, we relinquish our struggle to Him who alone has the power and compassion to bring us into our destiny.

Within the Most Holy Place was one piece of furniture, called the Mercy Seat, guarded by cherubim on either side of it. The Mercy Seat was significant because of the pulsating glow of unapproachable light that rested on the Mercy Seat itself. This pulsating light signifies the Presence of God as He sits on His throne in Heaven, signified by the Mercy Seat on earth. This Most Holy Place is a shadow of the reality in the spirit realm and corresponds to the throne room of God. His throne, as it exists in Heaven, is the Mercy Seat in the Most Holy Place of Moses' Tabernacle.

His throne,
His final resting place,
is in your heart.

From His throne, God rules, blesses, heals, shows mercy, and generally conducts the affairs of His Kingdom in every dimension. Can you see why it is the Love Shack? It is a place where David was not afraid to enter, for he knew the heart of the Father and the fellowship of the Spirit. The actual Presence of God dwelled in the Most Holy Place. From His throne, the glory, power, and love of God was poured over the whole earth.

King David understood this incredible power and prayed for His Presence to consume the earth with salvation, redemption, and all that His Presence brings with Him. Healing, wholeness, destiny, purpose, hope, and fulfillment are part of the salvation of the Lord that flows from His throne. And His throne, His final resting place, is in your heart.

> *The Always-Present One has chosen Jerusalem. He wants* [it] *for His home.* [He says]*: "This* [is] *My resting-place forever. Here is where I want to stay. I will bless her* [with] *plenty of nourishment. I will satisfy her poor people* [with] *food. I will let her priests receive deliverance. And, those of her who follow* [God] *will truly sing for joy!* (Psalm 132:13-16)

YOUR HEART IS THE LOVE SHACK

The secret is out. *Where* is the Love Shack? It is in you. *What* is the Love Shack? It is your heart. The place of wholeness, love, mercy, forgiveness, and hope is your heart, the throne of God on earth. Jesus says:

> *"Listen, I stand at the door. I am knocking. If anyone hears My voice and opens the door, I will come inside with him. We will have dinner together. I will give the right to sit with Me at My throne to the person who conquers as I conquered, and as I sat down beside My Father at His throne"* (Revelation 3:20-21).

Most have been taught since they were young children that Jesus comes and takes up residence in our hearts when we come to the Lord. Is that true? Are our hearts the thrones of God? You may remember the little drawings in the *Four Spiritual Laws* booklet published by Campus Crusade for Christ. The drawings show the throne in our hearts as either occupied by you or your Lord. The good news: it is true. Jesus takes up permanent residence in our hearts. It becomes His throne on earth. We become the temple of the Lord.

> *Surely you realize that your body is a temple sanctuary? You have received the Holy Spirit from God. The Holy Spirit is inside you—in the temple sanctuary. You don't belong to yourselves* (1 Corinthians 6:19).

> *Guard what you were trusted with through the Holy Spirit who lives in us* (2 Timothy 1:14).

DARE TO EXPERIENCE THE LOVE SHACK

Allow Jesus to live His life through you. He does not want you to guess about what He would do and then attempt to do it. He wants you to yield to Him so He can do what He actually wants done. I can always tell when I am trying to serve Him as opposed to yielding to Him. When He is moving through me, the results are creative, exciting, way out-of-the-box, and visible. They leave me, as well as the one I am talking to, with a sense of peace and righteousness. The breeze of His Presence blows gently and tangibly over the situation and we know that God has spoken.

In the Love Shack, be ready to serve instead of being served. Be ready to give rather than receive. Accept being last to finish a race so you can help someone else finish first. When you help someone win, you win too, even if you are not in the race.

Well-known pastor and author T.D. Jakes prepares us to serve:

> Come down from the lofty perches of superiority and wash the feet of the hurting. There are no differences in the feet of the washed and the feet of the one who washes them. They all look the same. Your ministry truly becomes effective when you know that there is precious little difference between the people you serve and yourself. Then and only then have you laid aside your garments![2]

WHAT YOU HAVE ALWAYS WANTED

So now the question is simple, "What now?" For years you have been working to get closer to your Lord. No matter what you did, nothing seemed to work. You wanted to be in a place of fulfillment and peace with the Lord. You wanted your insatiable hunger and thirst for Him to be filled, but it never happened. So it was easy to conclude that He simply didn't want you. Maybe you decided that you were an anomaly of nature, that the desires you had were impossible to satisfy. There was no choice but to live with this shortfall and pretend it did not exist.

There is a problem with that logic, however. It is difficult to find something that is not lost. How many times have you determined that something was lost only to have your spouse, child, or coworker pick it up right in front of you? It was there all along, but you could not see it. The frustration was there not because it *was* lost, but because you *believed* it was lost. As soon as your eyes fell upon the thing you lost, the frustration was gone.

He has been working to get your attention all this time.

I am here to tell you that nothing is lost. I am here to tell you that He did *not* reject you or give up on you. He is *within* you. He has been living there since the first time you called upon Him, and probably before that. He has been working to get your attention all this time. But you, like so many others, believe the things taught by people who have never seen the Lord or felt the wonder of the eternal tug on their hearts for more of Him. That tug is Him. He wants your attention so you will finally see that He is with you. He will never leave you. He has so much to tell you and so much for you to experience. He already dwells within. Stop looking for the forest among the trees. You already have what you yearn for. Meditate on this thought. Think about what you truly want in a relationship. Talk to Him. You will be pleasantly surprised to sense that He is near; that He hears you; that He is responding to you. Just listen....

Follow your heart. Believe what the Holy Spirit is saying to you. Dare to believe the song that is in your heart.

Dare to live in the Love Shack.

Chapter 8

EMBRACING UNION WITH GOD IN THE LOVE SHACK

I pray not only for My apostles, but also for the people who believe in Me through their teaching. May all of them be united, just as You are in Me and I am in You. I pray that they will be in Us, so that the people of the world may believe that You sent Me. I have given them the glory that You have given Me. May they be united, as We are; I in them and You in Me. May they be completely united, so that the people of the world will know that You sent Me and that You loved them as You loved Me. Father, You loved Me before the world was created. You have given Me glory. I want them to see it. I want them to be with Me, where I will be (John 17:20-24).

REVELATION IN THE LOVE SHACK

The several books I've written on my journey to the Love

149

Shack have helped me, and others, determine what was happening in my heart. Chapter 19 of *Romancing the Divine* offers some of these insights:

> You would certainly think that once a person had responded to the wooing love of the Lord to join Him on the seat of ultimate mercy, it would be the end of the journey, or at least the end of the search.
>
> But this is only the end of the beginning, for there is so much more. Now, however, the search is with the Lord and not for the Lord. Destiny is in process, not in limbo. Now you can walk with the Lord in the cool of the morning instead of wondering where He is in the gloom of night.
>
> For the Lord whom I serve had suddenly come to His temple, my heart, the holiest place of all. I discovered that I really love doing the work of the Lord. Before the revelation, *I* was doing the work. It was remarkable. He never called me to work for Him or to act like Him—He called me to simply say yes to Him so that He could freely live His life through me.
>
> But as usual, I got it all messed up.
>
> Secretly I really did not want to say yes to Him, so I devised all kinds of ways to appear as though He was living His life through me when really I was only pretending to be yielding to Him. I knew His voice; I just chose to ignore it. I preferred a shallow life as opposed to responding to His leading deep in my heart. In those days, I was the

one in charge of things. Now, by His mercy, He is the One in charge. He is the One who makes the decisions.

Things are much different in this dimension of the Love Shack where I voluntarily lay down my will for His. In this place, I live in the conscious decision that I have once and for all yielded myself to Him.

But in the Holy Place, the dimension fraught with humanity in all its idiosyncrasies and selfishness, every decision turns into a major argument between the flesh, the Spirit of the Lord—and sometimes the enemy. That kind of arduous struggle always wears me down. It saps me of strength and time. It clouds my spirit and makes it difficult for me to hear Him say anything. I am most happy to say that those days are somewhat behind me.

I am looking forward to saying yes to Him regularly, daily, even moment by moment. In the long run, it is certainly much easier, much more peaceful and fulfilling.

Living in the yes of God changes my responses to life's circumstances and the leading of the Lord. I have already determined that I have nothing to lose and absolutely nothing to argue about. Now whenever I come to one of those frightening walls I do not want to face, I simply remind myself that I have already made the decision to agree with Him, no matter what.

I do not really know what life will hold beyond my fleshly humanity, beyond the veil of human control. However, I am certain that His plan for me, His desire for me, is far better than my own meager attempts for meaning and ultimate fulfillment.

I simply remind myself that I have already made the decision to agree with Him, no matter what.

The Lord gently broke into my thoughts. Suddenly all the sounds and activity of heavenly worship rushed into my spirit. He had my full attention.

"You should not be surprised to feel things more strongly than you have ever felt them before. Now you will begin to feel what Father feels. Everything Father feels, He feels passionately and completely. He does not fear emotion, for it is the overflow of His total commitment and determination to draw humanity to Himself. It will certainly be a new experience for you, and it may be a little unnerving."

No sooner had He spoken than I caught a glimpse of the Light that had escaped the Most

Holy Place when the Lord first entered the torn veil. It continued its boundless journey through the ages, touching every time and every nation. It was not a haphazard flash of light, but a calculated, methodical search for everyone who ever lived. Upon each one, the Light of His Glory rested, urging, nudging, calling, drawing each person to Him who sits on the throne.

I sat in awe of the Light's gentle determination to shine in the heart of every person, revealing the love and forgiving power of the Christ of God. I found myself captivated with its work. I watched as the Light approached each heart. I found myself praying on the breast of Father on behalf of these people I did not even know. I held my breath in anticipation as His love poured into the hearts of folks in every epoch.

I prayed fervently as I saw so many turn in rejection of the Son. I wept as I witnessed the Light shut out of so many lives. My tears of intercession turned the Lord back toward those who had rejected Him only moments before. Some melted before Him on repeated attempts to break into their lives, but many, so many, did not. I turned my body on the Mercy Seat to get closer to Father as I prayed. As I did, I realized that I was not the only one who was in fervent intercession. In fact, the prayers I prayed flowed out of the endless compassion of the One who gave Himself for those who were now deciding to reject His eternal love and compassionate mercy.

I wept as He wept.

I prayed as He prayed.

I was as overwhelmed with love as He was.

Every sound we made, every cry we cried, moved the heart of Father. He did not need to hear words, for every groan from the deepest place in our hearts reverberated with the mercy, the grace, and the desire of the Father.

Words only hinder the power of His Spirit, cluttering the air with human desire and fleshly, mental gymnastics in our frail, earthly attempts to solve each one's dilemma as they, too, wrestled with their own humanity. No, words were not at the heart of genuine intercessory prayer.

I watched the Lord and yielded to Him. I understood that He needed me only to agree with what He already knew needed to be done. My participation caused eternity itself, and the plan He had determined, to flow effortlessly into the dimension of the five senses. It is here where His work is accomplished. It is here where His love is displayed through you and I who live only to please Him and to be found in the center of His marvelous activity on this planet.

Eternity flowed into time and space as I found myself groaning in prayer with intensity I never before imagined.

Never before had I increased in faith as I lived in intercessory communion with my Lord.

Never had I spoken less and said more.

Never had I seen more and understood less.

Never had I been so content.

Never had the joy of the Lord been so wonderful as I agreed with Him, watching angels pour into the dimension of mere mortals, coming to the aid of flesh and blood.

The activity was beyond description.

The determination was beyond explanation.

The love was beyond comprehension.

Some responded in a moment of time. Others allowed the light of His glory a bit of room within them, preserving the hope that His love would ultimately overpower the no that resides within all of us. One thing was certain—salvation began to work in the heart of humankind the moment we began to search for Him who is Truth. And salvation continues to work in the hearts of all long after we determine in our heart of hearts to yield to His love, His purpose, and His destiny.

Countless myriads responded to Him as He cried throughout the ages, throughout all time, "Eye has not seen, ear has not heard, neither has it entered into the hearts of man all that I have prepared for those who love Me."

Many believed. Many came to Him. Many felt the wonder of His Presence as His light shone brightly into their hearts, warming them to the depths of their beings.

The more people melted in His Presence, the more faith rose within me. I found myself pressing against Him with anticipation of what would happen next in response to this mortal man's prayer.[1]

KNOCKING ON YOUR LOVE SHACK DOOR

As discussed earlier, a Christian best-seller becomes that because readers are hoping to discover a secret, a hint within the pages that will help them in their quest for destiny, fulfillment, and answers to some measure of true spirituality, no matter how that may be defined.

It is sad when you don't get what you hoped for. But when wishes comes true, [it is like eating] fruit from the Tree of Life (Proverbs 13:12).

Everything you have hoped and dreamed can be reality in your life.

The Lord never intended to offer hope without delivering it in its fullest reality. The pages of this book were written to help you understand that everything you have hoped and dreamed can be reality in your life. Everything your Lord has dreamed for you is real and is waiting for the right heart, the right prayer, the right time, the right faith, and the right hope. Let me briefly explain.

THE RIGHT HEART

*People who have pure hearts are happy, because
they will see God* (Matthew 5:8).

There is no doubt that God is looking for pure hearts. But
God's definition of pure is different from ours. We consider the
pure in heart to be those who are perfect, without fault, without
sin, and sometimes even without temptation. There is, however,
great news. God's definition of purity of heart requires repentance,
honesty, and truthfulness in your heart. When we fail, we fail.
When we give in to temptation, we give in. We are not condemned
for that. But if we do not repent, we cannot return to hearing His
voice clearly. Many times we make excuses for why we act the way
we do, blaming someone else or convincing ourselves that we are
merely victims of circumstances beyond our control. The result is
a heart that is harboring sin and unrighteousness.

Impure motivations are another major reason we have impure
hearts. We should be serving the Lord for His sake and His sake
alone. We do not serve Him for fame, money, or influence. We
serve Him because we carry in our hearts the pure desire to give
Him glory and to let His name be known in all the earth.

Fortunately, none of these conditions are fatal and none need
to affect the rest of our lives. We are taught to pray for understanding so that we can see the condition of our hearts and repent
of those things that keep us away from the purity we want.

*O God, examine me and know my heart. Test me
and know my anxious feelings. See if* [there is any]

157

bad trait in me. Lead me in the everlasting way
(Psalm 139:23-24).

*Create a pure heart for me, O God. And renew a
solid spirit within me* (Psalm 51:10).

So purity is a condition of repentance, softness of heart, and
willingness to hear things about ourselves that may not be so good.
It is not so much what we do that is wrong, for we all fall short in
ourselves, but it is how we handle our failures and our need to be
seen and respected. The blood of Jesus cleanses us and keeps us as
pure as our repentance allows us.

*The blood of Jesus cleanses us and
keeps us as pure as our repentance
allows us.*

You [are] *my Hiding Place. You protect me from*
[my] *troubles. You surround me* [with] *songs of
victory* (Psalm 32:7).

Yes, in Christ we find the perfect hiding place, where the
enemy cannot get to us and our flesh cannot overpower the desire
of our hearts to keep following the Lord in spite of our failure and
brokenness.

THE RIGHT PRAYER

You mean there is a right prayer? It is amazing how folks fog up the spiritual atmosphere with fleshly, faithless prayers. We often pray out of panic, anger, and fear. This kind of prayer is seldom what we really want to say, but we say these prayers with such conviction that our spiritual space is cluttered with mixed signals and words we eventually wish we had never uttered. Of course God is gracious and full of mercy and forgiveness, so it is best to offer repentance as soon as we realize what we have done. That clears away the fog and helps us see from His point of view.

The right prayer is a prayer of single-minded confidence and assurance that He knows what He is doing. If we are certain that we know what we want to do, then we should pray with confidence, in our spoken language as well as the language of the Spirit. We pray and then we are thankful as we patiently await the right time. A lifestyle of worship and thankfulness that He is working out His plan is not only emotionally healthy, it is spiritually powerful in keeping our spiritual space crisp and clear.

THE RIGHT TIME

Time is an experience of our dimension. It is not an experience of eternity. The ancient prophets prophesied about time that they knew not, yet every promise has an appointed time of fulfillment. God is never late. Jesus died at just the right time. Only the Father knows the time of the final curtain call on life as we know it now. Multidimensional people—us—need to understand that it is easier to see something than it is to wait for it to come.

We once drove through Casa Blanca, New Mexico, where the Rockies stand tall and majestic in the distance—they certainly define "purple mountain majesties." The shock was in discovering that the distance to the base of these mountains was more than 50 miles! We were sure they were much closer because of their size. We saw them from afar before we actually reached them.

Time cannot help us, but it surely can fool us. I remember believing that the publishing of a book, the preaching of a sermon, or the arrival of my ministry onto the scene was critical to the furtherance of God's Kingdom. Although we all have very specific callings, whether in traditional ministry or another career—we are *always* in His service—the Kingdom of God does not hang in the balance until we show up on the scene. I often think of the boy lion, Simba, in the movie *The Lion King*. His song "I Just Can't Wait to Be King" is a reminder that God does not want us in the battle until He says we are ready. Better to stay where He has put us, serving Him in whatever our hands find to do in all faithfulness and with a servant's heart, than to run ahead of Him and risk shipwrecking our life's work for many years to come.

Better to stay where He has put us, than to run ahead of Him and risk shipwrecking our life's work.

You are the only one who can ultimately determine the times and seasons for your own life. You should seek the prayerful counsel of those you trust, but *you* must carry the responsibility for your actions.

THE RIGHT FAITH

No one can do what God wants done. We are not capable of the works of God. When we try to accomplish something alone, apart from God, the results are awful: Adam and Eve fell from Eden; Abraham fathered a child who would torment God's people through the ages; and Peter was rebuked by Jesus for trying to bring in God's Kingdom apart from the Cross (and a Roman guard lost an ear). Knowing that He has everything under control and His will is being done is our best assurance that His plan will unfold at the right time. Your quiet confidence gives clarity to His voice and His leading so you can hear and respond with assurance—through faith!

THE RIGHT HOPE

Pure hope in God is a basic belief in His goodness. It is a child-like peace of mind that He is in control. With single-minded hope in Him, you will naturally, eagerly keep the ears of your spirit alert for His voice. You will live in a mindset of readiness, unencumbered by things that would make it impossible for you to follow Him wherever He may lead you. Although you need to be personally responsible for yourself and to all those who look to you for love and support, hope keeps your thoughts straight and your mind at rest.

You *know* He will come through for you.

Chapter 9

LIVING IN THE LOVE SHACK

I pray that victory will come to Israel from Mount Zion! May God give back the prosperity of His people! [Then the people of] *Jacob will rejoice.* [And the people of] *Israel will be glad* (Psalm 53:6).

God shines from Jerusalem, the beauty of which is perfect (Psalm 50:2).

Like most believers, you have spent your entire life trying to get close to the One you love. Your time, energy, anointing, and most of your strength have gone toward the goal of being close to Him. Also like most believers, when you read verses like the following they seem too good to be true:

However, God was rich in mercy, because of His great love which He had for us. While we were spiritually dead in sins, God made us alive with Christ. (You have been saved by God's gracious love.) And God raised us from spiritual death and **seated us in the heavenly world** *with Christ Jesus. God wanted to show the superior riches of His gracious love for all time. He did this by using Jesus to be kind to us* (Ephesians 2:4-7, emphasis added).

We say we believe the Bible, but do we really get it? We have difficulty really understanding what Jesus meant when He said:

There are many rooms in My Father's house. I would have told you, if that were not true. I am taking a trip to prepare a place for you. Since I am leaving to prepare a place for you, you can be sure that I will come back and take you with Me, so that you will be where I am (John 14:2-3).

Truth is multidimensional. It transcends the limited intellect of the human mind.

We are slaves of the five senses. When the five senses do not confirm what we believe or what we hear from God, we simply reject it. We have been trained to accept the input from the fleshly realm as the whole truth, when it is *not* the whole truth. Just because we don't see something or sense it, does not mean it isn't so. The whole truth is discerned by the input of the natural *and* spiritual realms and all other dimensions of living.

Once we understand that Jesus really is living within us and that we are the throne of God on earth as the Scriptures say, everything begins to change.

We have been limited in our comprehension of who we are.

Reality is far greater than we have been led to believe. Truth is multidimensional. It transcends the limited intellect of the human mind. Science has discovered parts of the brain that are not being used. They have surmised that at some point in our past, we used a much larger portion of our brain. They speculate that something happened over time that has caused us to use less of our brain than we used long ago. But I believe there is another explanation. Maybe we were created with a larger capacity brain because the time would come when we would need it. Maybe God knew we would grow into needing this unused brain capacity as we grew and learned and discovered over many, many millennia. But all that is for another book.

I want to make the point that we have been limited in our comprehension of *who* we are, *where* we are, and even *why* we are. We so desperately want to experience the Lord, but we have missed the reality of God's greatest mystery. We have been locked into a single dimension while being multidimensional beings. We have not allowed contrary thoughts to challenge the status quo. We have been taught that heresy is closer than we think. We have been convinced that we do not have the capacity to discern the voice of the Lord or to be led by His Spirit. Our faith has been "dumbed down" by those who want to preserve their position, their power, and their pension.

But the truth is out. God made all of us with the capacity to hear, understand, and take responsibility for what God has called us to and all the dreams He has destined for us. I can hear God. We can all hear God. All of His children can hear Him. We can all be led by His Spirit. We are multidimensional beings made to move and live freely in a universe blessed with wonders far beyond our imaginations, just waiting to be discovered, enjoyed, and put to use for the purposes of God on earth.

As you quiet your soul, you will begin to hear His voice loud and clear. He does not play games with you. He does not play hide and seek. He wants you to live in the Spirit. He wants you to know, comprehend, and walk freely in all He has for you. Your quiet times need to be just...quiet. You and I need daily lifestyles of meditation, sensitivity, and openness to the Holy Spirit. He is constantly speaking, but unfortunately, not many are listening.

A Dare You Can Grow With

All we imagine and want from the Lord is done and in place. We need to become spiritually minded, spiritually sensitive, as well as faithfully and eagerly attentive to His Spirit.

You will be amazed at what opens to you! But you will need to be willing to hear things that are completely different from what you are used to hearing. Dare to go beyond your past and current experience. Dare to go beyond your doctrine, your theology. Your experience with the living God depends on your courage to go beyond your safety zone, the limited view of the horizon that prevents you from seeing over to the realm of all-God.

All you desire from the Lord is done and in place.

By choosing to live in the Love Shack, you have made the incredible discovery that *you are* the holiest place in all of the universe. This is not because you are perfect. It is not because you don't "drink, smoke, chew, or run around with people who do." It is because He has taken up permanent residence within your heart. You are willing to see things you have never seen before. You do things you never thought possible.

You have also discovered the place of intimate exposure. God sees you for who you are—and loves you unconditionally. What a relief! You never have to hide from Him again. He knows you. He sees you. He understands you. No more excuses. No more lies. No more deception. He absolutely knows everything about you. You have disrobed the fleshly words of religion. You have abandoned the carnal parlor tricks to try to get God to serve you. Now He really sees you in all your humanity. He sees the good, the bad, and the ugly. And He loves you, gathers you, and calls you to sit with Him on the Mercy Seat—His throne in your heart.

THE LOVE SHACK IS FOR LIVING

Now life really begins. The bleak life of religious repetition is finally over. The depressing struggle with uncertainty has come to an end. Finally you experience what Jesus promised, "...I came, so that they might have life—to the fullest!" (John 10:10). This "fullest" is much more than we can imagine. We are free from the weight of human worry and fear. We can see. We can understand. We can believe. The random lifestyle so many live with every day disappears when we see the perfect order, directed desire, steady love, and certain resolve He has toward us. The weight of sin and fleshly work that saps our strength and robs us of our joy is replaced with the certainty that everything we do really has a purpose. The joy of the Lord is truly our strength.

The joy of the Lord is truly our strength.

Jesus said and still says to us, "You are tired and have heavy loads. If all of you will come to Me, I will give you rest. Take the job I give you. Learn from Me because I am gentle and humble in heart. You will find rest for your lives. The duty I give you is easy. The load I put upon you is not heavy" (Matt. 11:28-30).

Who would not want to release their uncertainties, pain, and weight of guilt to Him who has nailed our cares to the Cross? Now these very familiar verses take on new life and new hope. You can see the determination in His eyes and feel the passion in His heart toward all who call upon His name. For all races, all nations, and throughout all time, He draws, loves, heals, restores, and sends them into the destiny for which they were born.

SEATED WITH HIM

As you walk toward Him and turn around to sit down beside Him, for the first time you will see what He sees. Seated with Him, you will see all that you have had your back turned away from your whole life. Now everything changes. Now you see life from His perspective. You discover what you have ignored in your own journey to His Presence.

How do we make it from one day to the next in our own strength, wisdom, and grace? Seated with Him, His love, grace, and strength pour out from you like a gushing waterfall. You can't believe what you have been missing! You have been living with spiritual blinders on for so long, but no more!

You have been content with the partial for too long. You have been content in your minimal experience for so many years that you have adapted quite well to its utter deficiency. Your doctrines have changed to accommodate it. You have forced many wonderful New Covenant provisions into that indefinable dimension called the millennium. But all that has changed now.

From His view, life apart from the fullness of the New Covenant provision is not possible. You desperately need all that Jesus purchased for you. Your spirit groans with emotions too deep for words. The flighty quoting of Scriptures and the flippant recital of a positional doctrine in Christ will no longer suffice. To win—and God does want you to win—there must be a total fulfillment of the New Covenant deep within your heart. His first appearing as your Sin-Bearer and Healer brought you to this point. But now you need more; you need Him if you are to win. Now you see it. Now you know it is possible. Now you know you can win!

THE LOVE SHACK IS FOR LOVING

As the secrets of living in the Love Shack are revealed daily to you by your heavenly Father, your life become more and more enriched. The following is what I wrote in *Secrets of the Most Holy Place, Volume One*, Chapter 12, as these secrets were revealed to me.

> Again you abandon your heart to His will and eagerly look toward His full manifestation. He is not going to bear sin again. He is going to be bearing the salvation of the Lord, a dimension beyond the veil, an experience of the third day, a relationship that will transcend both gifts and abilities. This encounter will cause your heart to overflow with His love and mercy. As His strength wells up within you, your voice rises above the clamor of religious confusion and inner tyranny.
>
> "I can do all things through Christ who

strengthens me." Though you have heard this verse a thousand times before, only now does it deposit inner fortitude and resolve into the very center of your being. Previously you had only mouthed the words—today you are experiencing them. "I can do all things through Christ who is my Strength. Through Him I can run through troops and leap over a wall." And in the course of it all, you will never even come to a sweat, for it is not you who must labor. It is He who accomplishes His work within you.

He is pouring out His joy and the oil of gladness upon His people, that they might be the planting of the Lord, trees of righteousness, bearing fruit in every season and constantly bearing green leaves upon their branches, leaves that will heal the nations.

You understand more fully than ever now. You are not healed for your sake alone. You are not delivered only for your own well-being. Jesus has redeemed you, healed you, and delivered you, that you might be a yielded vessel through whom He might minister the fullness of His salvation to the earth.

He has set the prisoners free. He is binding up the broken-hearted. His Presence is comforting all those who mourn. He is pouring out His joy and the oil of gladness upon His people, that they might be the planting of the Lord, trees of righteousness, bearing fruit in every season and constantly bearing green leaves upon their branches, leaves that will heal the nations.

And He gives all this, not just for your sake; not so the Church can close herself off from the rest of humanity, spending a lifetime pouring the same water into each other's vessels; not so she can maintain a level of wholeness or shield herself from the hurting millions who need bread to eat, water to drink, health to be restored, and hope to plant. No, it is Christ who will, through you, restore what the cankerworm and palmerworm have eaten. It is you who will restore the old waste places.

So, be happy, O you people of Jerusalem. Be joyful in the Always-Present One, your God. He will do what is right, and He will give you the autumn rains. He will send you abundant showers, both the autumn rain and the spring rains, as before. And the threshing-floors will be full of wheat. And, the barrels will overflow [with] new wine and olive oil. "I was the One who sent My great 'army' against you people. Those swarming locusts and the hopping locusts, the stripping locusts and the gnawing locusts ate up your crops. However, I will make it up to you for those [bad] years. Then you will have plenty to eat, and you will be satisfied. You people will praise the Name of the Always-Present One, your God. He has treated you wonderfully. My people will never be shamed again! Then you will know that I [am] in the midst of Israel, and that, I, the Always-Present One, [am] your God. There is no other [God]! And, My people will never be shamed again!" (Joel 2:23-27)

Even in your brokenness—in fact, only in your brokenness—do your hands drip with His oil and your cup overflow with His living water. You will restore the ancient ruins. You will recover the people lost to generations of desolation. One word from your lips will deliver a person unto the Kingdom of His beloved Son. You will reclaim what the enemy has claimed. You will deliver to the Lord what past generations have allowed to disintegrate. Your hands, your words, your acts of love, oozing with His Presence, shall restore a generation to the Lord. With untold joy, you realize that it is not too late to experience the fullness of your salvation.

Yes, it is clear now. Very clear. You were never called to merely go to Heaven. You were called to minister from within the veil of the Most Holy Place, your personal Love Shack. You were called to be redeemed and to redeem. Your life now is to flourish with His life. How could you have missed it? To be converted merely to maintain and hold on until the end was never His intention for you.

With untold joy, you realize that it is not too late to experience the fullness of your salvation.

You have only begun to experience the fullest measure of the New Covenant. You have only begun to touch the rest of the New Covenant reality. No longer will you be part of a whimpering, impoverished, and frightened Church. No longer will you cower in the corner, hoping for Jesus to come and rescue you out of your troubles. No longer is your hope merely in Heaven. It is now with Him who indwells you with might and power.

Now you know that He did not bring you this far just to abandon you. His deliverance is complete. To spend the rest of your days where you have been would be like the children of Israel never entering the Promised Land. The desire of God's heart was never to only deliver Israel from Egypt! His intention was twofold.

His plan was to bring them out of Egypt and into Canaan, out of bondage and into the land flowing with milk and honey.

We have tried too hard to maintain life so far below His salvation! We have ignored the second part of God's provision! He never intended that we merely be delivered from sin and its terrible bondage. And He will not give up until we have stepped into the Promised Land, where real intimacy begins and His life subdues ours.

Within the veil, this total salvation begins to show itself in real ways in your life. Now everything looks different from how it once looked. As you are seated with Him, looking out over the vastness of humanity, even the Church takes on a new dimension. It looks immensely different as you look at it from His vantage point. In fact, you are dumbstruck at the abruptness with which your vision and understanding of the Church has changed.[1]

THE LOVE SHACK IS FOR SERVING

Now that you've come this far, you are acutely aware of the depth of God's love for you and His desire to be with you always. Come with me into the Love Shack as I share the last chapter in *Romancing the Divine* with you:

As I leaned against Him there on the Mercy Seat praying as I was inspired by my Lord, I heard the voice of the Father.

"Go," was all He said.

"Go," He repeated.

Was He talking to me? I did not want to go anywhere. I was content to stay where I was, nestled close to Him in prayer. Surely He was talking to someone else, someone who did not pray as I was praying. Surely He needed me to pray. He needed me to break into eternity and rend the heavens so that which was eternal could flow into time and space. Surely...

"Go."

Surely He meant for me to stay where...

"Go."

But who would pray? Who would stand in the gap for those who needed Him and needed to be...

"Go."

"OK! I will go! I will go. Yes, I will do what You want me to do." I turned to the Lord Jesus, who sat with me as I prayed. "I will go, but I do not want to leave the Presence of the Father."

The Lord gave me a surprised-look smile. "I did not say you would leave the Presence. I simply said to go."

Seeing my perplexed look, He continued, "Do you think I was alone as I walked among men? Do you think I was alone as I ministered to the masses and healed the broken of body and soul? Did you really think that 'go' meant that you would have to leave His Presence to do His will?"

"Well, I don't know. I mean, of course not. I would really go, I guess. But how would I do His bidding if I did not leave His Presence?"

The Lord looked at me patiently without responding.

I stared back...rather vacantly, I might add. It is an odd silence when the Lord is looking at you, waiting for an intelligent response. But I am not really so dense. Finally it came to me.

"I get it! I will go but never leave His Presence!" The Lord smiled with relief. "I get it. Saying 'yes' means I do what He wants. So I go where He is going so He can do what He wants to do through me."

"You do get it!" the Lord laughed. "You never have to leave the Presence of the Father. Simply go where He is going and do what He is doing. You will change everything around you without even trying."

"Let's go!" I shouted, suddenly filled with a fresh sense of faith.

We were gone before I realized what was happening. I followed Him from place to place, from mountain to valley and back again to the mountain. I was doing things I never knew I could do. He took me to places where I never thought I would ever see Jesus going, and there I was with Him. Amazing.

"I should be afraid someone will see me here," I laughed to the Lord. "I could get into big trouble, You know. I might ruin my witness!"

We laughed together. I realized that the only witness I have is He that lives within me.

"Well, if anyone asks me what I was doing here, I will say that You sent me and that You came along." We laughed again.

"My, my, my, Lord!" I chuckled uncontrollably. "What is happening to me?" Tears of joy streamed down our faces.

This "yes" of God was far from the predictable religious behavior I had been used to for so many years. This was far more exciting and far more rewarding. People were actually responding! There were no tricks, no gimmicks, no religious fads to lure a tired and bored humanity, a tired and bored church system. There were no little books scaring people into doing whatever you wanted them to do. These people were really falling in love with Jesus! They were actually following Him because they wanted to follow Him!

This "yes" of God was far from the predictable religious behavior I had been used to for so many years.

I struggled to speak through my laughter. "Oh, Lord, I cannot believe it." I had to wait for another attack of laughter to wear down before I could continue.

"I would normally have to spend hours coming up with spurious Bible studies to explain why most of what we did had no fruit. Oh...my...I cannot control this." My eyes were watering with joyful mirth. "Oh my, Lord. I am sorry. I guess this is not very funny."

He did not answer so I looked to where He was standing. When our eyes met, we both once again broke out into uncontrollable and most certainly non-religious laughter.

Again, I had to work to recover. "Lord," I finally was able to speak, "what would people say if they knew what we were laughing about? They would be so offended."

Giving me a deadpan look, the Lord said, "Many people would be offended if they saw Me laughing about *anything*."

"Lord, I cannot believe You said that!" We laughed together late into the night. I must have been dreaming, but I knew I was not. I was enjoying time with the One I loved.

Times were certainly different. How liberating to be able to respond to the Lord and not to others or their expectations of me. I was free to do only what *He* wanted. My future belonged to *Him*. My times were in *His* hands. My goal, my passion, my joy was now simply to say "yes" to Him every day.

Would I mess up again? Would I fall occasionally into sin? Unfortunately, but honestly, yes. But I am living with Him in the Love Shack where mercy and grace run freely and forgiveness strengthens me to move forward. The stench of sin wants me to carry guilt and live in depression, but I have experienced His love. I will not go back to guilt. I will not go back to shame. To be sure, each failure is a humbling experience. I realize how weak I am. I get frustrated, and I wonder how He can endure my weakness another minute, especially when it seems as though I fail again and again.

My goal, my passion, my joy was now simply to say "yes" to Him every day.

But I know in whom I have believed and I am persuaded of His love. He is not only able, but He also wants to forgive me and empower me to go on. He wants to fulfill His destiny for me.

He knows I am just dust. I know I am just dust.

He knows the love He has for Me. I am discovering the love He has for me.

He knows what I can do. I am discovering what I can do.

He has dreamed a dream for me. I will, by the grace of God, fulfill the dream He has for me.

I am becoming more and more convinced that if God is for us, who can be against us?

Who will bring a charge against me? Who has the right, who has the authority to separate me from my Lord? Who has the right to tell me I cannot be forgiven until I go through someone's concocted plan of religious gymnastics? Who has the right to stop me short of His glory? No one.

I am sure that nothing will be able to separate us from God's love which is found in Christ Jesus, our Lord—none of these things—death, life, angels, rulers, the present time, the future, powers, heights, or depth! (Romans 8:38-39)

I am hidden in Christ, covered with His blood, held by His love at the Mercy Seat of His throne. There He continuously loves me, forgives me, empowers me, and causes me to live in the "yes" of His purpose.

He has romanced me.

He holds me.

He keeps me.

I do not have to convince Him to love me or desire me or be patient with me. He is all over me with desire and love and patience.

This is certain: The Lord whom I have spent a lifetime romancing, was romancing me all along. The One I was trying to win had already been won, without any effort on my part.

It was true love from the very beginning.

It will be true love until my final breath.

Then, it will be true love for all eternity.[2]

Conclusion

You have a choice. I have a choice. All of God's children have a choice to make.

We can choose to live in the warm and embracing Love Shack where He is Lord of all we think, do, dream, desire, are, and will be. Choosing to reside in the Most Holy Place gives us a perspective about life that sets us free—now and eternally. Satan cannot huff and puff and blow his way into our Love Shack because we are completely protected by God's love, and His blood covers the entrance.

The Love Shack is the place Adam and Eve abandoned. They chose to leave their lovely haven and reside in a cold and lonely world where murder, hate, abuse, and strife reign. While in the Love Shack the first couple was free to be naked and not ashamed, free to be all that He created them to be—joyful, loved, healthy, honest, content, successful, well-fed, prosperous, surrounded by beauty beyond belief.

How many of us have thought, *If only Eve would have stood strong against the serpent's deception and had not tempted her husband to disobey God. But, gee, if I were Adam or Eve, I would have probably done the same thing.*

But on this side of Eden and the Cross, we *do* have a choice—we *can* stand strong against the evil one's deceptions and temptations. We can choose not to live in our familiar doctrine-padded refrigerator boxes in the back alley of His creation. We can choose not to keep that hidden "thing" in the closet, just close enough to feed our fleshly desires. We can choose not to venture into satan's snares that keep us chained to self-promotion, greed, lust, and hate, which torment our spirits and souls and eat away at our physical bodies.

Choosing to live in the Love Shack not only provides the structure in which you and your heavenly Father can laugh and love and live life to the fullest, it also becomes your place of peace—the peace that your body, spirit, and soul cries for amid the everyday trials of work, home, marriage, children, bills, health problems, and the rest of what we experience in this dimension.

In the Love Shack you can freely run with the angels, laugh with the Father, go fishing or shopping with Jesus, and welcome the Comforter into your boardroom, classroom, and bedroom. It won't take you long to realize that this is life as it was meant to be. This is how living is supposed to feel—exhilarating, exciting, enormous!

Step into the Love Shack, pull the door shut behind you, and hear the blood of Jesus splash against the roof, covering all you ever did against your brother, sister, parents; covering all you ever said against your friend, enemy, coworker; covering all you ever thought against your spouse, boss, or children. Hear the blood splash over all you ever did and will ever do that goes against His Word.

You are forgiven…you are safe…you are His one and only you.

So, here's to living happily ever after in the Love Shack with Him.

I know that this life is for you. I know your heart—it is just like mine!

Endnotes

CHAPTER 1

1. Donald Miller, *Blue Like Jazz: Nonreligious Thoughts on Christian Spirituality* (Nashville, TN: Thomas Nelson, 2003).

2. William P. Young, *The Shack: Where Tragedy Confronts Eternity* (Los Angeles, CA: Windblown Media, 2007), 95.

3. Stephen and Alex Kendrick, *The Love Dare* (Nashville, TN: B&H Publishing Group, 2008), back cover.

4. *The Love Dare*, 91.

5. Rick Warren, *The Purpose Driven Life: What on Earth Am I Here For?* (Grand Rapids, MI: Zondervan, 2002).

6. http://www.purposedrivenlife.com/en- US/AboutUs/ AboutTheAuthor/AboutTheAuthor.htm); accessed 12/22/08.

7. http://www.leftbehind.com/05_news/viewNews.asp ?pageid=929&channelID=17); accessed 12/20/08.

8. Tommy Tenney, *The God Chasers: My Soul Follows Hard After Thee* (Shippensburg, PA: Destiny Image, 1999).

9. John Eldredge, *Waking the Dead: The Glory of a Heart Fully Alive* (Nashville, TN: Thomas Nelson, 2006).

10. C.S. Lewis, *Mere Christianity* (New York: Touchstone Books, 1996).

11. John Bunyan, *The Pilgrim's Progress* (New York: Dover, 2003).

12. John Bunyan, author; Jim Pappas, adapter, *Pilgrim's Progress Part 2: Christiana* (Shippensburg, PA: Destiny Image, 2005).

13. Don Piper, *90 Minutes in Heaven: A True Story of Death and Life* (Ada, MI: Baker Pub. Group, 2008).

14. *Mere Christianity*, 99.

15. Paulo Coelho, *The Alchemist: A Fable About Following Your Dream* (New York: HarperCollins, 2006).

16. *The Love Dare*, 1.

17. *The Shack,* back cover.

18. http://www.nimh.nih.gov/health/publications/suicide
-in-the-us-statistics-and-prevention.shtml); accessed 12/22/08.

19. *Blue Like Jazz*.

20. *The Alchemist*.

21. *The Alchemist*.

22. *The Alchemist*.

23. Tony Dungy, *Quiet Strength: The Principles, Practices, and Priorities of a Winning Life* (Carol Stream, IL: Tyndale, 2008), back cover.

24. *Blue Like Jazz*, 217.

25. Joyce Meyer, *Battlefield of the Mind* (Boston: Hachette/FaithWords, 2002), 101.

26. Myles Munroe, *God's Big Idea* (Shippensburg, PA: Destiny Image, 2008), 214.

27. Bruce Wilkinson, *The Prayer of Jabez: Breaking Through to the Blessed Life* (Multnomah, 2005), 17.

28. T.D. Jakes, *Release Your Anointing* (Shippensburg, PA: Destiny Image, 2008), 74.

29. *Battlefield of the Mind*, 332.

30. *Waking the Dead*, 241-242.

31. Don Nori Sr., *Romancing the Divine* (Shippensburg, PA: Destiny Image, 2006), 187-188.

CHAPTER 2

1. *Romancing the Divine*, Chapter 3.

CHAPTER 3

1. *The Shack*, 66.
2. *The Shack*, 179.
3. *Romancing the Divine*, 152-155.
4. *Romancing the Divine*.

CHAPTER 4

1. Don Nori Sr., *Tales of Brokenness* (Shippensburg, PA: Destiny Image, 2002), Chapter 14.

CHAPTER 5

1. Don Nori Sr., *Secrets of the Most Holy Place, Volume Two* (Shippensburg, PA: Destiny Image, 2005), Chapter 5.
2. *Secrets of the Most Holy Place, Volume Two*, Chapter 1. Related Scripture references: Matt. 28:18-20; John 3:16 NASB; 1 Cor. 1:29 NIV; Matt. 6:10; John 6:56; Matt. 5:14-15.
3. Don Nori Sr., *The Power of Brokenness* (Shippensburg, PA: Destiny Image, 1997), Chapter 15.
4. *Secrets of the Most Holy Place, Volume One*, Chapter 16. Related Scripture references: Ps. 25:15; Matt. 4:17; Mark 1:1-4,15; Luke 3:3-4; Exod. 3:14; Matt. 22:32; Mark 12:27; Luke 20:38; Heb. 3:7,15; Matt. 23:27; Matt. 6:6.
5. *Secrets of the Most Holy Place*, Postlude. Related Scripture reference: 2 Tim. 4:8.

CHAPTER 6

1.   Don Nori Sr., *The Angel and the Judgment* (Shippensburg, PA: Destiny Image, 1996).

2.   *Romancing the Divine*, 179-181.

CHAPTER 7

1.   Oswald Chambers, *My Utmost for His Highest* (Uhrichsville, OH: Barbour Publishing, 1991).

2.   T.D. Jakes, *It's Time to Reveal What God Longs to Heal: Naked and Not Ashamed* (Shippensburg, PA: Destiny Image, 2008).

CHAPTER 8

1.   *Romancing the Divine*, 173-178.

CHAPTER 9

1.   *Secrets of the Most Holy Place, Volume One*, Chapter 12.

2.   *Romancing the Divine*, Chapter 20.